MW00679642

Kathryn Molavu
10/2001

Life's Little Lessons

A GUIDE BOOK
TO GET YOU THROUGH

KATHRYN MORAVEC

Sunstar
PUBLISHING LTD.

Life's Little Lessons
A Guide Book to Get You Through
by Kathryn Moravec
© United States 1999

Sunstar Publishing, Ltd.
204 S. 20th Street
Fairfield, Iowa 52556

First Edition 1999

Printed in the United States of America

Library of Congress Catalog Card Number: 99-68056

ISBN: 1-887472738

Cover Design, Irene Archer
Book Design, Irene Archer

The information in this book is meant to be a blessing. However, this information is not medical advice. Neither the author, nor any persons or organizations associated with the author, are in any way liable for others or any effects resulting from practicing this information.

Readers interested in obtaining further information on the subject matter of this book are invited to correspond with:

The Secretary, Sunstar Publishing, Ltd.
P.O. Box 2211, Fairfield, Iowa 52556
More Sunstar books at: http://www.newagepage.com

This book is dedicated to all the souls who have chosen
to improve the world by starting with themselves
and to my husband Alex for this belief in me.

CONTENTS

ACKNOWLEDGMENTS

I would like to acknowledge the individuals who in one way or another assisted me in the writing of this book. My husband Alex for his ability to quietly listen when I need it most, and for his love and moral support I love you with all of my being. My children, Alex, Steven and Shauna, you always give me reason to look at life from a fresh perspective—You are so precious to me. Daniele DeVoe and Beth Sanders, my first two teachers, now friends, without your help I never could have arrived at this point, I am deeply grateful to you both. To all my family, especially my mom, and friends I would like to say that you assisted in my development, and I thank you for standing by my side through the laughter and the tears. I would also like to thank all of the souls who have touched me at some point in my life, for you too have assisted me on my path of self discovery. Ultimately, I am grateful to God for the never ending flow of love that encircles me always!

I have changed the names and unimportant details in the examples throughout the book to protect the identities of the individuals.

PROLOGUE

*T*his book is intended for anyone who has wished for a compact guide on life. I do not claim to be an expert or guru, or to have all the answers. The information contained in this book is not new but, you will find it expressed in a user friendly format.

The material is derived from my own personal experiences, teachers I have studied with, and Divine Guidance. My goal is to provide you with tools that can enhance your life experience. Please open your heart and your mind as you read, and take only what you feel you need from this book. It is my firm belief that we all will end up in the same place, each on our own path. Any path you choose is the correct one for you. The only difference between paths is the adventure and the time when each of us arrives at the destination. I hope this book will assist you on your journey, and that it can help you avoid getting stuck on the side of the path. Enjoy!

INTRODUCTION

> *Every experience we encounter attempts to teach us something.*

*L*ife is a continual learning and growing process. I began my spiritual journey on a conscious level when I hit rock bottom. It was one year after my second divorce, and the relationship I was in seemed to have more downs than ups. I always believed that if you were a good, kind and genuinely caring person, things in life would work out. I tried to be kind and caring, but felt that I must be doing something wrong, because I couldn't for the life of me make a relationship with a significant other work out.

> *One day I finally had enough and screamed at the Universe:"IS THIS ALL THERE IS?" I found this to be the point where the Universe, God, Goddess, Source, what ever name you use, wants us all to get to. We have to be open to receive guidance, and sometimes, actually most times, you have to be emptied first. Every experience we encounter attempts to teach us something.*

I was sent two wonderful teachers whom I now call friends.

They are two very different individuals and came to me exactly when I needed them. I have read from the Bible, old texts and other books written by individuals on their spiritual journeys. You may think that you only want to improve yourself in your present life, not start a spiritual journey. I am here to tell you that any self improvement is a step on your spiritual path. I believe that we all originate from the same Source, which to me is God, Goddess All That Is. (I also refer to them as the Universe.)

I do not judge others because of their belief system nor ask anyone to share my beliefs. As I stated in the prologue, I believe all paths are correct. If you do not care for the words I choose to use such as God, Goddess All That Is, then substitute your own words for mine. Please do not get hung up on the verbiage because it is not the words but, the message they relay that is important. I also believe that we co-create our life with God.

> *We have free will but, the Universe will allow you only so much time to achieve wisdom before it steps in.*

What I mean is that if every experience is a lesson and if you do not learn it, the Universe will readjust your situation to see if perhaps you will get it another way. Good examples are my two divorces. I had relationship lessons to learn. Even though each succeeding relationship improved, the problems remained similar.

At the rate I was going, when I found the man of my dreams I would be too old to even remember why I wanted him in my life.

> *You had better learn something from each life encounter or you will continue to repeat the lesson with different faces and places attached to it.*

Co-creation is further discussed later in this book.

With the help of my two teachers I was able to grow in consciousness at a very rapid rate. Although I found the information from my teachers and the books I read to be valuable, I struggled in applying the knowledge to my life!

> *It is easy to tell someone to love unconditionally, to forgive, and to "know oneself" but how does the individual accomplish it?*

After many trials and errors, tears, and plain frustration, I learned the how. The way in which I achieved growth may or may not be the path for you. My intention is to impart the Universal basic truths that I learned, and show you how to apply them to your life. If my way is not your way you can still learn from my experiences, and apply the truth to your life in your own manner.

I again ask that you open your mind and heart as you read, and realize that you are about to embark on a wonderful journey of self discovery. Thank you for allowing me to share in your adventure!

1

THE SELF

The place we will start is with you. You are embarking on an exploration of the self.

> *The majority of people go through life blaming everyone and everything outside themselves for their pain, restlessness, frustration, and failures.*

They tend to repeat their mistakes or recreate the same situations because of their refusal to look inside themselves for the answers. They live their lives thinking they have no control, power, or choice.

Everyone needs to learn that there are always options to be chosen in every situation. We all have access to the same exact amount of personal power.

> *Personal power gives us the ability to make choices, to feel confident and strong, and to find peacefulness within ourselves.*

Once this is realized, all you need to do is to acknowledge the truth that you are a strong and capable individual, and embrace your power by making life choices and feeling good about them. We perceive power as something given to us by money, position, or other people. This is false power, because it can be taken away or lost.

> *True power comes from within, goes everywhere with you and can never be taken away by anything or anyone.*

> *We can and do give our power away!*

This occurs when we allow others to make our choices, or when the opinions of others have too much influence on our decisions. When we allow money, personal possessions and social status to become of prime importance to us, we have also given our power away.

As children we are taught that putting our needs first is considered selfish. I know of no one who likes being called selfish, so we sacrifice our own needs or desires because we think that someone else's are more important. It seems that in the process of pleasing everyone such as family, friends, coworkers, and bosses, no one ends up happy, not even ourselves.

I am not suggesting that we never please others. What I'm saying is that we must learn to honor ourselves first, and then we can honor others.

> *If our cup is empty how can we expect to fill anyone else's cup?*

When we honor ourselves it means that we accept each aspect of who we are, including our dark and hidden parts, without change. It also means that we make choices regarding our life that are for our own best and highest good.

> *Life is too short for us to live only for others—we must all do what brings us joy, which can and will include service to others, but not at the expense of ourselves.*

In a moment we will discuss how to release our undesirable traits but first I would like to explore the ideas of victim and martyr energy.

Victim Energy

Victim energy is when an individual feels they have zero choice in any situation. I am not talking about individuals who have suffered from a crime. I am speaking about people who think that life happens to them and they are unhappy with the outcomes. These individuals feel helpless and hopeless.

Martyr Energy

Martyr energy occurs when a person chooses to do something and then proceeds to complain about the hardship it caused them. People in martyr energy are typically unhappy.

As a society we need to come together and heal the victim and martyr energies as they are very counterproductive.

How can I say that you must accept yourself without change, if I am going to show you how to change?

> *You must accept yourself completely right now as you are, then you can begin to eliminate the traits you feel are no longer a part of the person you wish to become.*

If, for instance, you choose to reduce your weight, you do not delay self acceptance until you reach your target weight. You accept yourself now and continue to accept yourself all through the diet.

Self improvement occurs because of a desire to grow. If we waited to accept ourselves, until we felt we were the absolute best person we could be, we would never reach acceptance.

> *We cannot honor that which we do not accept.*

> *The self is divided into an emotional, mental, physical, and spiritual body. Each body has a purpose for existing.*

The goal is to understand each body and bring all four into balance. I believe this is a lesson that everyone must go through and that it is a difficult and continual process. This particular lesson took me over a year to understand and to complete the initial phase.

With this chapter, I intend to walk you through the steps so that you can accomplish your balance at a pace that is comfortable for you. I will define the different bodies, beginning with the physical body and moving through the rest. To help you I will also include a few, certainly not all, traits or questions associated with each body.

Physical Body

> *In trying to change ourselves, the physical body is where most people begin.*

This is because the changes are visually apparent to yourself and to everyone else. The physical body also encompasses our environment including our work, home and the entire planet.

The physical body allows us to experience life through our five senses of touch, taste, hearing, smell and sight.

> *There are no two individuals completely alike—even identical twins have differences—which means that every experience is unique to the person.*

Our body is a wonderful vehicle no matter what size, shape, sex, or color it is. It does not matter where we live, how we look, or what type of job we hold. We are all created equal with variations that make us unique individuals. This keeps life interesting!

TRAITS: Weight, status of health and fitness, type of work, debt, possessions, environment—cluttered, messy, clean.

Mental Body

The mental body determines how we perceive our world. It processes all the incoming information and determines what is important to us.

> *The mental body also strives to keep our lives from changing by creating fear of things that are new or different.*

Our ego resides in the mental body. Its function is to protect us from the world at large and from learning who we really are. The ego uses fear to keep us from growing. To countermand this we need to embrace change, silence our ego, and not allow fear to rule us.

TRAITS: Controlling, manipulative, judgmental, worry, calm mind, fear of anything.

Emotional Body

The emotional body allows us to feel our world. Our society has taught us to suppress our emotions. Generally women are taught to quell their anger, and men their sadness.

> *There are only two true emotions: love and fear!*

All other emotions such as compassion, joy, satisfaction, anger, frustration, guilt, shame, etc. are forms of either love or fear. We need to understand why we feel the way we do, then accept the emotion being experienced.

> *Once you accept your emotions you can use them to move through situations effectively, rather than having your emotions use you.*

No one can make you feel one way or another. You alone are responsible for the way you feel. If you are sad you should allow yourself to cry, and feel the sadness fully. When you embrace or feel the emotion, you can then release it.

> *We are divine spiritual beings designed to live in joy.*

We are meant to feel all emotions, but we were never meant to hang on to the fear-based ones for long periods of time. Keeping negative emotions alive for months or even years will eventually cause harm to the physical body. Chapter Five delves into this further.

QUESTIONS: Do you shut your emotions down? Are you too emotional, allowing them to rule you? Are you hanging on to guilt, shame, grief, frustration?

Spiritual Body

The spiritual body is the one that drives us to discover why we exist.

> *It is interesting that our Soul knows why we are incarnated to this earth plane, even if our conscious mind does not.*

Compassion, intuition and unconditional love reside in this body. To assist us in our growth in consciousness our Soul uses the spiritual body as a tool, a way to communicate with us. This is often the most neglected of the bodies.

QUESTIONS: What are your beliefs on life and death? Are you solid in your beliefs? Do love and compassion emanate from you?

Male/Female Energy

Everyone embodies both male and female energy. Male energy is on the right side of our bodies and is represented by the sun. It is electric, active, and giving. Female energy is on our left side and is represented by the moon. It is magnetic, receptive, and creative.

> *Concepts or ideas are conceived on the female side and brought to fruition—into the physical world—by our male side.*

Now that you have an understanding of each body's functions, you can begin to analyze them to discover who you are deep down inside.

> *You must be totally honest with yourself, which can prove to be very painful and hard but ultimately satisfying.*

To begin your analysis find a quiet place, free from disruptions. Examine each of your bodies and see what you like and dislike about each one. It would be helpful to write your list down. Take your time in doing this assessment as it is important for you to identify every aspect of each body. Move through this exercise at a pace you are comfortable with, as it is not a race and no one is timing you. Do not be surprised if you find this to be the most difficult and tiring thing you have ever done. Remember you are doing an honest analysis of who you are, so write everything down. This is for your eyes only, and you do not need to share it with anyone unless you choose to.

> Most individuals never delve into their essences; instead they define themselves from the outside by their roles in life: mother, father, wife, husband, child, sibling, executive, laborer, boss, employee, etc.

We all hold a variety of roles, each role being only a fraction of who we are as a whole. When we define ourselves from the inside instead of from the outside, we still hold the various roles, but we are able to be a whole individual in each one.

> Being whole all the time actually makes life easier, because as the roles change, we do not.

Do you now see why being totally honest with your self assessment is so important?

Begin to Heal

> The next step is to heal the areas you are uncomfortable with or that you feel impact you negatively, and to enhance the attributes you are pleased with.

Examine your list and decide which attributes or traits you choose to eliminate. After you have identified what you choose to eliminate, you must first embrace the trait and understand how it has served you up to this point in your life.

> *Each aspect of who you are has a reason for existing.*

An example of this concept is in my past relationships with my significant others. I tried to become who they thought I should be and maybe who I thought they wanted me to be. I denied parts of myself because I thought it would make them happy. I wasn't happy, but that was okay, because I knew that if I kept on giving, and being who they wanted me to be, the relationship would be fine. (I think there was a bit of martyr energy in me way back then!)

The relationships all failed, so what led me to choose this type of behavior? It took much searching, and being very honest with myself to realize that I was engaging in a behavior designed and implemented by me, to prevent me from being abandoned.

> *Deep down inside I was terrified of being alone, so I developed a trait that I thought would protect me—that is, letting other people define who I should be.*

Over and over again, it didn't work.

Once I understood why I acted this way in relationships, it was easy to embrace the trait, then release it with love.

> *I reclaimed my power and embraced myself wholly.*

Now I am with a man who is wonderful and kind, and best of all he is in love with the real Kathryn.

We will use guilt as another example of how a trait can serve you. It doesn't make too much difference as to why one feels guilty. It could be because of something they did or did not do. How does guilt serve? It is a form of self-punishment.

> *Most individuals believe that if you do something wrong, you have to pay a penalty before you can be forgiven.*

Guilt may appear to be a small "price to pay" but in reality it shrouds one's entire life, choking out joy, peace and happiness. Knowing that guilt is self-imposed pain allows you to embrace it, then release it with love because the guilt did what it was created to do.

Please, be patient with yourself as it may take some time for you to understand why a particular trait came into being.

> *It takes deep probing to figure out how the trait has served you and you must take full responsibility for its existence.*

You and you alone are the reason it was created. You can't blame anyone else...oh, you can try, but in doing so you render yourself powerless.

> *You are the ruler of your destiny.*

Once you discover why the trait is part of you it becomes very easy to heal.

> *Everyone is able to heal themselves, with the right tools.*

I have used the following five steps to release the traits I felt I no longer needed. I found the exercise to be simple, relaxing, and beneficial. Don't "freak out" when you read the first step and see that you need to meditate. Meditation is not a horrible, boring task and you do not need to spend hours doing it, but it does take practice and patience.

> *You will find that meditation when done correctly can increase your energy level because it helps to clear your mind.*

To achieve a clear mind you need to allow your thoughts to come in and then move right on out. Do not dwell on the thought. If you resist your thoughts from coming in they will bombard you. This is why you allow them to enter your mind, then leave. The meditation in the Appendix creates a Quiet Place for you to go. The place you create is yours and can be anything from a beach, to a meadow, or a favorite childhood hangout. You can use this space for relaxation, release, healing, or to tap into your inner guidance. Make your space beautiful, unique, and sacred.

> When you release a trait or habit you do it in the energy of love.

You will send the trait out from you into the universe, surrounded in your love. Then you replace the released trait with a positive one in order to fill the void. The new trait is admitted into you in the energy of love, and must be nurtured in order for it to thrive. I suggest that you release one trait at a time because you must integrate the new energy and there is no point in overdoing it. Begin.

Exercise

1. Do Quiet Place Meditation. (Appendix of book)

2. Once you are in your Quiet Place visualize the trait you choose to release. Give it form, color, texture.

3. Embrace the trait; hug it, and thank it for doing the job it was created to do. In your mind or out loud tell the trait that it no longer serves you to keep it.

4. Release the trait with love, throw it out to the Universe.

> Visually see the trait leave you and dissolve into space.

5. Visualize the void left by the trait. Fill the void with a pos-

itive trait: give it form, color, and texture; if you can't think of a positive trait use joy, or unconditional love.

> *Visualize the new positive energy entering the void and becoming part of you.*

When you release a trait or a habit it is important to involve your physical body as much as possible. See and feel the trait, or habit, then be aware of how you feel once you release it, and how you feel when you embrace the new trait!

> *Releasing the trait will not magically change everything in your life. You still need to work on incorporating the new energy and find new patterns of behavior.*

You eliminated the energy and the reason for the old attribute and the old patterns. The released trait may resurface in situations and at first it will be confusing to you. Like an onion with many layers the released traits may be hiding deep inside.

> *As you grow in consciousness you are actually peeling your layers off and you may need to release the attribute again, but it will be on a different energy level.*

When you recognize this phenomenon occurring all you need to do is repeat the above exercise.

You have embraced, released, and incorporated your chosen traits. Now you must embrace your past and embody it into your foundation.

> *This is important because your past shapes, creates, and forms the building blocks of the person you are now.*

If you do not integrate your past lessons into the foundation of your Being, you will repeat them. You are not integrating the emotions of the lesson, only the facts and what you learned from it. We must truly learn from our lessons to the point that the message is embedded within us.

> *When you disregard the past, you leave holes and thus you are not whole.*

Look at your past with joy, and love, because it has brought you to where you are today.

> *Defining who you truly are is an arduous task but lessons do not need to be hard and learned with great difficulty.*

You can choose to have your lessons presented with grace and ease and in the energy of joy as your teacher. Even if you do only the exercises described in this chapter and none of the other ones outlined in this book, you will still be way ahead of the game. You will find that the rest of this book centers on you and how you interact with the world around you.

A few thoughts as we close this chapter.

> *Compare yourself only to yourself.*

We can always find someone we consider better or worse off than us, but the only true measure of growth is to oneself.

> *Examine your life and know that you helped create it.*

Take responsibility for your life choices, thus eliminating victim and martyr energy. Other people will impact your life, but you hold the power on your response to the situation.

Embrace who you are!

> *You are a unique individual...one of a kind!*

If you don't love yourself how can anyone else love you?

The foundation is now laid for your continued growth. Congratulations!

2

UNCONDITIONAL LOVE

Y ou have explored your inner self, released and embraced chosen attributes. You are now going to learn how to love yourself and others unconditionally. Unconditional love seems to be the new buzzword, but what does it mean, and how do we achieve it?

> *Unconditional love is pure, accepts self and others without change or agenda, and is based in the energy of honesty, trust, freedom, and forgiveness.*

To practice unconditional love you must eliminate expectation, obligation, limitation, and judgment, while embracing honesty and forgiveness. This love is for yourself, others, and life. I bet you are thinking that this could mean quite a bit of work on your part, and you would be correct. Let's look in detail at what unconditional love is and is not. I will explain each aspect and guide you on how to eliminate or embrace it.

Expectation

Expectation occurs when we decide in advance how we want a person or situation to be.

> *Many individuals plan their entire life out in detail, including how they expect their partner, friends, family, coworkers, or experiences to be.*

They also will project how they themselves will behave or what they will feel in particular situations. Personally, I used to plan a decade in advance, and I am thankful that I no longer am a planner.

Here is an example of how people plan and expect:

You decide that you and your significant other (S.O.) need to spend some quality time together. You plan in detail a night out for the two of you. You think about the date all week, become excited with anticipation, and you know that your S.O. will be thrilled. The day arrives and you go on your date, but as the date progresses things do not flow exactly as you planned, which dampers your enthusiasm. Perhaps your S.O. doesn't appear to be as thrilled as you expected, which deflates you another notch. At the end of the evening your S.O. tells you that he loves you and is touched that you would go out of your way to spend a night out with him. You know that they didn't like their meal and they mentioned that the movie was just okay. Not the response you were looking for?

> *The fact that things didn't meet your expectations probably left you feeling unappreciated, and you no doubt missed the important detail that your partner loves you and was happy just to spend time alone with you.*

Does any of this seem familiar to you?

> *Expectation causes us to feel sorry for ourselves when situations or people fail to measure up to our lofty plans.*

When expectation is placed upon ourselves it can drive us to become a workaholic or an overachiever, bulimic, anorexic, depressed, sometimes even suicidal. Why then would anyone choose to keep expectation alive in their life? Because it's expected…(just a little humor).

If you think you would like to make your life and the life of those around you easier, eliminate expectation.

> *The best way to eliminate expectation of self, others, and life is to live in the moment.*

We live in the physical world so we must make plans, but we can do so without attaching expectations to them.

> *Allow life to progress moment by moment, permitting it to be what it is.*

Without expectation everything becomes new and wondrous because you are able to submerse yourself in life without the worry of figuring out how it will unfold.

Obligation

> *Obligation occurs when we do something we do not want to do, because we feel unjustified responsibility.*

Obligation is a bitter pill to swallow, and all you achieve for your efforts is frustration, anger, or guilt.

> *To release obligation all you need to do is honor yourself.*

Others may view this as being selfish, but in truth it is living in honesty.

We touched on honoring yourself in the first chapter, and now I would like to elaborate. Determining if you are honoring yourself or being selfish is simple. The distinction is related to the intention, motivation, or reason behind your thoughts, words, or actions.

> *You honor yourself when your choices are based in the energy of harmlessness and love.*

Everyone will benefit from those decisions in one way or another. If your choices are based on the premise of how you alone will profit without regard to the effect it will have on others, you are being selfish. If your choice is not what another may want it to be, then how can the choice benefit them? This is a very good question and I will use an example to answer it. Sally asked her husband Jeff to attend a lecture with her. Sally knew that Jeff wasn't interested in the topic to be presented, but she didn't want to go alone. Jeff knew that Sally would be upset and disappointed if he said no, so he said yes. Jeff regretted saying yes and felt angry that Sally would even ask him to go with her. By the time they arrived at the lecture Jeff was showing his resentment. Sally really wanted him to have a good time and focused her energy on trying to please him, which caused her to miss most of the lecture. Care to guess how the rest of the night turned out?

Sally and Jeff would have benefited more had Jeff declined the invitation, instead of accepting it to please Sally. By saying yes out of obligation Jeff managed to create misery for the two of them. If Jeff had said no, Sally still could have attended the lecture, and shared her experience with him later that night.

> *Individuals may attempt to use manipulation to get you to do what they desire.*

It was okay for Sally to ask Jeff to go with her even though she knew he wasn't interested, because Jeff possessed the power to say yes or no. If Sally used manipulation to get Jeff to go, and that is why he said yes, then neither of them honored themselves, or each other.

That's right, you can just say no. It is almost too easy. Own your personal power and create choices for yourself.

You can and will continue to do things for other people, but it will be because you choose to.

> *Living without obligation frees you to be joyful in everything you do.*

Limitation

> *Limitation is propagated by the mind, through the use of fear.*

Our mind tells us to fear change, because it does not want us to grow. We limit ourselves and others based on "what ifs." "What if" I fail, "what if" he leaves, "what if" I get fired, "what if....?" These are all examples of fear-based thinking.

> *We all want guarantees in life, and there are none.*

You can "what if" life to death, or you can escort the unknown into your life. God and Goddess are limitless, so how can anything created by the Universe be limited? Learn to think creatively, enormously and with imagination.

> *Imagination is your window to the true reality.*

If you can reprogram your mind to accept all things as possible, you will open doors that were once closed. When you eliminate limitation, the roles of victim and martyr are erased as well. Every situation you encounter will have more options available for you to choose from.

> *Do not allow your mind to use its limits against you.*

Instead use your mind, as the tool it was intended to be, and bring into form a life free from fear and limitation, and filled with choice and abundance.

Judgement

Judgment arises from, you guessed it, our mental body. Our brains are able to absorb vast amounts of information and, out of necessity, they developed a system to filter the incoming data. Every single piece of data is logged and filed away for future use.

> *Our minds sift through the incoming data daily and produce an opinion about its value to us*

The mind determines if the information is good, bad, or neutral to our situation.

Many things play a key role in the development of our filter system, such as family, school, community, personal experience, friends, television, and the media. The list goes on. If you are raised in a family and community that promotes racism, odds are you will be a racist. This is not because of your own assessment of the practice, but because older, respected individuals have shared their judgments with you and thus begun the development of your filter.

We judge an individual based on his or her skin color, length of hair, mode of dress, actions, and ideology, just to name a few.

> *Situations or experiences are judged on the bits of data we are able to gather either first or second hand.*

People have used judgment as a means to keep one group in power over another, and to ensure that the "have" and "have-not" groups never mingle.

> *Judgment creates separation.*

Individuals worldwide have incurred a profuse amount of harm through the use of judgment.

> *The Bible tells us "judge not lest ye be judged" and I think it is great advice.*

Judgment infers that all things are not equal.

> *Things can be very different and yet remain equal.*

A pound of gold is equal to a pound of feathers, if you were judging weight. White is equal to black, which is equal to yellow, which is equal to brown, which is equal to white and so on. I am now speaking of the human race: we are all the same just different. (Again a little humor).

Have you ever been wrong in your judgments? Perhaps a rotten incident, at a second glance, became the best thing to ever happen in your life. We can never see or know the entire truth about an individual or any given situation. Assuming the above statement is true, I proclaim that the time has come for us to eliminate all judgment. You might question how we are to make decisions if we can no longer use judgment to determine if something is good or harmful for us? This is another very good question and the answer is that you use discernment versus judgment.

I define judgment as forming an opinion using emotion and no objectivity.

> *My definition of discernment is to form an opinion honestly, in harmlessness, and using all the facts available to you.*

When you use discernment you assess everything and you are aware of your filters. This enables you to move past them if need be.

Here is an example of using discernment instead of judgment. There is a young woman driving down the road and she spots a hitchhiker dressed in dirty clothing and who appears to be rough around the edges. It's raining and cold outside. Do you advise her to stop or keep driving? Really answer this question. What filter was on for you? Judgment would say, tell her to keep driving as we all know the dangers of picking up hitchhikers, especially if you are a woman. Discernment would request more facts. The new data is that the hitchhiker's car broke down as he was returning from his job as a welder. Discernment says pick the man up, as he needs help. There are always more facts to be known.

> *Judgment rarely seeks further input, it is usually an opinion rashly formed, often omitting all logic and obvious details that point to another way of thinking.*

Eliminating judgment does not mean that you like everything and everyone but, it allows you to be aware without being critical.

Forgiveness

> *Forgiveness is an expression that originates from the soul.*

When you truly forgive, you may remember the incident, but there will be no emotional ties attached to it. The incident will hold no power over you, because you will not feel the anger or pain.

> *If you still feel anger or pain then you have not released the incident with true forgiveness.*

> *Forgiveness allows us to be free and eliminates our excess baggage.*

The practice of forgiveness is for your own benefit, not that of the individual you are forgiving. Forgiveness can be done in silence and no one ever needs to know that you have forgiven someone. When we forgive it doesn't mean we must stay in the relationship, or in the situation, or ever speak to the person again.

> *It is a reflection of your acceptance of what occurred, and that you embraced the incident and the fear-based emotions that it led to, surrounded it in your love, then released it all to the universe.*

Healing can never take place until you learn and practice forgiveness.

In summary, I bet you are glad we have arrived here. This was an enormous amount of information for me to impart and for you to ingest. When you love unconditionally, you accept self and others without change. It is not unlike a mother's love for her child. You do not have to like the individual personality in everyone but you must unconditionally love the God Self that resides in all...no exceptions.

> *To love unconditionally you must eliminate expectation,*
> *obligation, limitation, and judgment from your life.*

At the same time disappointment, guilt, anger, frustration, fear, envy, and resentment are also eradicated. You will begin to design a reality for yourself, filled with acceptance, freedom, honesty, kindness, compassion, choice, joy, abundance, and internal peace.

> *Unconditional love must become a large part of your*
> *foundation if you are to continue your growth in*
> *consciousness.*

3
RELATIONSHIPS

*T*he previous chapters taught you to explore every aspect of who you are, to release the traits that no longer serve you, replacing them with traits you have chosen to grow with, and to love yourself and others unconditionally. The information contained in this chapter can be used to enhance every relationship you are involved in, including your relationship with yourself.

> *Until we learn who we are at the core, every relationship*
> *we encounter will reflect what is hidden within us.*

This is why I emphasize the importance of developing a solid, positive relationship with yourself first. Once you have achieved a nurturing and loving relationship with yourself all your relationships with others will evolve too.

As you progress you may find that some of your current friendships fall away. At first this is difficult to understand and to accept.

> *You made the choice to expand your being and identified the aspects of you that needed to be shed in order for you to achieve your desired growth.*

The same holds true for your relationships with other people—some may need to be cast off. The following is a good example of this:

When an alcoholic quits drinking he must make internal and external changes to maintain sobriety. He can't hang out with his drinking buddies, and most likely he will not choose to do so as the common bond of drinking has been severed. My husband Alex experienced this phenomenon when he became sober. Alex knew that he couldn't maintain his old habits and remain sober, so his group of friends gradually changed. This didn't happen because Alex suddenly disliked his old friends. The changes occurred because he became a new person and developed behaviors that promoted the new energy surrounding him.

Here is another less dramatic example: I have found on my spiritual path that I say good-bye quite often.

> *As you grow, you attract individuals to your life who complement you, and you release those who do not fit into your new way of being.*

It is painful to watch your friends slip away, but it is all part of the ever-changing cycle we call life. I am comforted in knowing that everyone is where they need to be, and if they're not in my life, I am grateful for the time we shared together. Don't get me wrong, it's not an easy thing to embrace and it has taken a lot of work on my part to reach this point of acceptance.

> *So when and if you find that certain ties are broken, be gentle with yourself—you will prevail.*

The relationships that remain intact will blossom.

> *It is far better to have one true genuine friend who enhances your life than to have twenty fair weather friends who are in your life for the good times only.*

To improve relationships with others you must always look to yourself first.

> *You take care of what's inside of you and the Universe will take care of what's outside of you.*

This is how to determine if a problem is in you or if it belongs to the other guy. You need to know that at times we project our feelings and problems upon another and that others will at times project their stuff upon us. When a problem in any type of relationship arises, examine yourself to ascertain if the problem is yours and is being reflected.

> *Do an honest self-examination and if it reveals nothing for you to work on, the problem most likely belongs to the other person and is being projected onto you.*

You then need to choose if you are going to walk away, or stay and assist them in fixing the problem. The decision is entirely up to you and will depend on the individual you are dealing with and what his relationship is to you.

> *Remember that to grow everyone must do his own work, just as you did*

This chapter will focus on significant other relationships because they tend to be the most complicated. You will be able to apply most of the information given to every other relationship you are involved in.

Why do we have so many divorces and breakups in America? I think there are a number of reasons, the first one being that we are unaware of who we are, and cannot know what we desire or need. Individuals enter into a relationship thinking the other person is perfect for them.

As the relationship progresses the individual starts to feel things are not quite right. Instead of looking inward for the reason for their discomfort, they look to their partner. The individual tells the partner that they are unhappy and requests the partner changes to accommodate their discontent.

> *The partner may make the changes, but it will be in vain, because the individual still lacks self awareness and change must always be chosen, not forced.*

> *Here is a basic truth: we make ourselves happy: Another cannot do this for us.*

Is it becoming clearer to you now, why self analysis was the first chapter in this book?

> *Another truth is that you must never change for another or try to change another.*

You can change yourself if you choose to. This is honoring yourself, without dishonoring another. I am not speaking of the little changes one makes to please their partner.

An example: When my husband and I began dating he was upset because I never locked my doors. Heck, I didn't even carry the house key with me. I moved from the big city to a small town, and felt safe without locking my doors. Alex grew up in the area, and he knew that crime can happen anywhere. It was a hassle to lock the doors, especially when I forgot my key, but I did it to please Alex. In turn, Alex hid a spare key outside for me, in case I forgot mine.

> *I changed a behavior but the behavior was not significant to me as an individual.*

If Alex had asked me to change my hair style, or to alter my personality, I would have had to say "NO," because those changes would have impacted whom I had chosen to be.

Relationships also fail because individuals confuse romance with love. Every good romance story contains drama, game playing, and a hero or heroine who saves the day. It works on soap operas, and in the movies, but it doesn't work in life.

To keep the drama alive you have to stay on a roller coaster. The ride can be fun for awhile, but becomes old very quickly. Balance and peace are innate to our nature.

> *How can you be balanced or peaceful when your relationship is continually seeking highs and lows?*

Romance has its good points, such as sending or receiving flowers, and spending a fun filled evening with your significant other. If you want romance in your life, create a romantic night, but don't try to live it every day.

> *Love is constant regardless of the circumstances.*

True love, loves on the "off" days as well as on the "on" days. Love doesn't care if you gain ten pounds, if you're crabby, sick, or relaxing in a tattered old pair of blue jeans.

> True love sees beyond the surface into the divine essence of the person.

> A third reason our relationships fail is that we are taught to seek out our complementary half.

This suggests that we are not whole individuals until we find a partner

> When we seek a relationship based on the premise of not being whole, we will find a partner who reflects a hidden portion of ourselves.

As you grow in consciousness, you will eventually embrace the part of you mirrored by your partner. When this occurs you no longer need the reflection, and this can lead to dissatisfaction with the relationship. You will desire to have another hidden portion of you reflected by your partner and they may or may not be able to do this. Most individuals are unaware of this growth process. They will verbalize their unhappiness, then proceed to say they do not know why they are unhappy, they "just are." The partner will often make statements such as "I don't know what you want from me."

> Again, I ask if you understand why we must always begin with the self, if we are to find peace and joy in our life?

As I stated, relationships are an outward picture of ourselves until our self work is done.

> *This is why you must always look inside yourself when you are dissatisfied or unhappy.*

You cannot look to another to be the provider of your joy, comfort, peace, or happiness, because they cannot supply it.

> *When you become solid in who you are, you find that everything you need is within you*

When you embody this, your relationships will no longer need to be a mirror for you. A good example of seeking contentment from another is reflected by Kim and Sam.

Kim constantly complained that Sam ignored her and that he was the cause of her unhappiness. Kim had various opportunities to develop new interests, and to go out and have fun with her friends. Sam never discouraged her from going out. Actually Sam was always delighted when Kim found something of interest to do. However, Kim chose to stay home, and wait for Sam to return from work, or an outing with his friends, so he could magically make her happy. Sam listened to Kim and really tried to please her, but his efforts were never enough, and after a time he quit trying.

Kim's lesson is very clear to see. Sam became the outward picture of how Kim treated herself. Kim's soul was pushing her to become whole, but she chose to ignore her inner voice. Once Kim begins to meet her own needs, her perspective on life will change because she will find joy and peace within herself.

Sam may or may not respond positively to Kim's changes. He is an individual with free will. Kim will still be happy because she created joy within herself.

> *The world is ready for the new energy of relationships, which is for each participant to be whole before entering into one*

The new approach is: two whole individuals form an unconditional loving partnership and together they create a path both will journey down while keeping their own identities.

Existing Relationships

The new approach to relationships is all well and good, but how do you apply the energy to an existing relationship? To begin we need to refresh ourselves on how unconditional love is lived. We discussed eliminating expectation, obligation, limitation, and judgment, in Chapter Two. We will now explore the energy surrounding unconditional love.

> *Honesty is a must.*

When you embarked on your self discovery, you needed to be honest with yourself. I found that being honest with myself was at times difficult, but when I was completely honest with myself, I couldn't be any other way with the world around me. I'm not implying that everyone is a liar, I'm just pointing out that we all, at times, hide the truth.

Why do individuals tell their significant other a "fib" or neglect to share certain pieces of information? Usually because they don't want to anger or hurt their partner. Sometimes it's to be cruel or to get away with stuff... Pure deceit... A partner may decide not to disclose their affair. Many will agree this decision is good, because while it unburdens one, it hurts the other, and for what?

> *I believe we need to live in honesty.*

The above dishonesty could cost an individual their life or their physical wellbeing.

> *The honesty may hurt emotionally, but it allows you to make choices that honor you and the pain does go away eventually.*

Being honest doesn't mean you are rude. You can use finesse, or "sugar coat" the truth if needed. An open, honest, relationship creates a space where you can share your feelings, thoughts, and desires safely. I know so many people who will share their body intimately with their partner but refuse to share their thoughts or feelings. These people then become upset, because their partner doesn't know how to please them. Why do we assume that our partners know what we want if we do not tell them? We must think that the world is full of mind readers.

Our mind has programmed us to fear honesty. Many acquaint honesty with vulnerability or weakness. We fear people will not understand or accept our opinions, ideas, or dreams and that we will be ridiculed or abandoned if we are honest.

> *Honesty has to be expressed at all times if a relationship is to grow.*

Trust is another essential component of unconditional love. To trust, one hopes or believes an individual will never harm them, physically, emotionally, mentally, or spiritually. Distrust in a relationship breeds jealousy, suspicion, and defensiveness. These are energy consuming emotions that are destructive to everyone involved.

> *Without trust a relationship can rarely survive, let alone thrive.*

We all seek freedom. In a relationship, freedom allows an individual to seek out new experiences or to participate in activities desirable to them, without repercussions from their partner.

> *Very few people enjoy being told what they can and can - not do.*

Freedom goes hand in hand with trust. If you trust that your partner always has your best interests in mind, they should be able to do or go wherever they choose. Freedom doesn't give you a license to betray your partner's trust.

> *With freedom goes the responsibility of making choices that will benefit both you and your partner.*

Lack of freedom can generate a lack of honesty and pent up frustration. Here are a few examples.

When Cindy married Joe she knew he loved to hunt deer. One year Cindy decided that Joe couldn't attend deer camp because she had things for him to do around the house. Joe was very displeased but felt he would "pay" dearly if he went to deer camp. During the week of deer camp Joe displayed frustration and anger because he wasn't doing what he really wanted to do. Cindy thought his "bad" mood was because of the chores she asked him to do, when it was really caused by his freedom being taken away. The best solution would have been for Cindy to let Joe know what she needed done and to allow him to choose the how and the when. Next Joe should have been honest with Cindy and told her how important deer camp was to him. They needed to reach a compromise, which we will discuss in a moment.

Becky knew that Greg hated it when she smoked, so she never smoked when he was around. She continued to sneak smokes at work or when out with her friends, and Greg found out. An argument ensued which could have been avoided if Becky had been honest with Greg and if Greg hadn't tried to restrict Becky's freedom. It is really very simple.

We already discussed forgiveness but it warrants repeating. Without forgiveness, honesty, trust, and freedom mean little.

> *Everyone, at one time or another, will do something that upsets or hurts their partner and they shouldn't have to pay for it forever.*

If the transgression is one so bad that you find you cannot stay in the relationship, then leave...but also forgive.

> *Unconditional love accepts without change, but to live in harmony we sometimes need to compromise and to agree to disagree.*

Each person needs to give in order to achieve a compromise. Everyone likes to do things his or her own way because it is the known way, but it is not always possible when you merge two individuals into one household.

When Alex and I married he had his bill and filing system and I had mine. I didn't care for his system, nor he for mine. We achieved a compromise. Alex's filing system was better, so we used it. He does all the filing, and I pay the bills. It has worked out very nicely for us both. The amount of time either one of us needs to spend on paying bills and filing has been reduced.

> *If anyone goes into a relationship hoping to always be agreed with, my advice to you is to develop a relationship with your mirror instead.*

It would be cheaper and take less effort on your part. It's wonderful that we all have opinions and that at times they differ from each other's. If you reach a stalemate, compromise cannot be achieved, and you are beating a "dead horse" you might as well agree to disagree. This is only a problem when a decision must be made. A possible solution to this dilemma is: When you know that a decision has to be made, agree before the discussion as to who will have final say.

> *When the relationship is based in unconditional love the decision made will benefit the whole, instead of promoting self interest.*

> *In summary, to develop positive relationships, you need to know yourself, and always honor yourself without dishonoring another.*

Seek your happiness and joy from within, and embrace the knowledge that everyone is already a whole being.

> *Live your life with unconditional love by embracing honesty, trust, freedom, and forgiveness.*

Apply this formula to every relationship you are in and you are going to find they will improve. This includes your relationship with your children, family, life partner, friends, coworkers and ultimately yourself.

4

OVERCOMING ADVERSITY

*I*n this chapter we will look at how you can find the light when things appear to be dark. We will look at overcoming the big obstacles that life places in your path. The next chapter will deal with the everyday demands of life. When you have completed this chapter I strongly encourage you to read Chapter Five as soon as possible.

Death, illness, and relationship breakups, all have loss in common.

> *We do not always know or understand the reason something occurs and most times it really doesn't matter.*

I will tell you, it isn't because you are a horrible person and a vengeful God is punishing you.

> *When tragedy strikes, no matter what kind, you need to move through the same basic steps in order to heal.*

The details of the situation do not matter, as a loss is a loss. When we experience a loss, we experience change, and with change comes loss. Loss of health, a body part, the functioning of our body or mind, death of a loved one, the ending of a relationship, are all huge losses to contend with.

> *We must grieve when a loss occurs in our life.*

Elizabeth Kubler-Ross described grief as a five stage process.

> *The five stages are Denial, Anger, Bargaining, Depression, and Acceptance.*[1]

Denial is the first stage, acceptance the last and the others have no particular order. The stages are pretty much self explanatory, so I will give you just a quick definition of them.

Denial is when you choose to believe that the situation is false. Individuals in denial will refuse to discuss any matter dealing with the true situation.

Anger, well what can I say? It is feeling hostile toward the situation and possibly the individual participants. Anger at God is not uncommon.

Bargaining is where an individual makes God a promise in return for the situation to resolve itself. An example would be: "I will never smoke again if you just let my father live."

Depression is a stage when the individual feels hollow, beyond sad, completely hopeless. This is considered a reactive and not a clinical depression because there is a cause for it.

Not everyone reaches the final stage of acceptance. Acceptance brings the individual an inner peace and calm.

---

[1] Barbara Kozier, Glenora Erb, "*Fundamentals of Nursing Concepts and Procedures, second edition*" (California: Addison-Wesley, 1997, 1983)

They know what the true situation is and they make rational choices for their future. As a nurse, I have cared for many patients and families who have refused to accept the situation they were in. Those same individuals were in a constant state of anger or depression which isn't healthy if sustained for long periods of time. When the facts could no longer be ignored, I found that the individuals experienced surprise and very intense sadness, maybe more so than those who achieved acceptance.

I found it particularly sad when the patient never moved into acceptance of their own death. The patient was usually terrified of dying and their fear made them unable to receive comfort from anything.

> *There is no right or wrong way to move through the process of grief, because it is different for each individual.*

It is important to know that we were never designed to harbor grief for long periods of time. Time frames are different for everyone. Just be sure that you are not stuck in the process of grieving and that you are moving forward every day.

> *Baby steps are better than no steps at all.*

I would like to first address relationship breakups. We're not going to discuss relationship failures, as I do not believe that we fail because a relationship ceases to exist. Our society teaches us to mate for life. If you find a significant other with whom you can grow, and be with for life, excellent. Unfortunately not everyone can achieve this. Statistics from the census bureau 1996 show that the divorced population is the fastest growing segment of our society. It quadrupled from 4.3 million in 1970 to 18.3 million in 1996.[2] We discussed the reasons why in the last chapter.

> *If you apply everything in this book, your relationship may still end.*

I have come to realize that we are not always meant to stay together forever, but you can heal the hurt and move forward. There is comfort in knowing that both of you came together to accomplish what you needed to as a couple, and parting allows each of you to continue growing on the path unique for you.

> *Every relationship has value, even the worst ones.*

Love felt and expressed is never in vain, regardless of whether the love is returned. If you can determine why the relationship ended or turned sour, chances are you will not repeat the same pattern.

I am no stranger to heartache. I describe it as the worst emotional pain you can feel and live. In my case, I swore that I would have to get better to die. I have cried enough tears to last two lifetimes...no, make that three. Do I have the magic cure for heartache? No! If I did I would bottle it and give it away.

---

[2] *Census Bureau 1996*

> *When you hurt, no one can say or do anything to make it better.*

My goal is to share what I have learned, to help you change your perspective and maybe make it easier for you to deal with your pain.

When you are suffering, feel your emotions to their fullest. Allow yourself to experience your feelings. If you ignore your emotions they will continue to surface until they are acknowledged.

> *Closure can only be obtained when all issues surrounding the situation are addressed.*

Remember that what we choose to let go, must be embraced before it can be released. Advice will be free flowing, so be sure you listen to your heart and heed only the advice that makes sense to you. If you are unable to release your emotional pain and you find that it is disrupting your life, you may need to seek professional help. Many times our well meaning friends and family will trash our partner, trying to make us feel better. It's okay to be angry, but assigning blame gets you nowhere.

> *True love never turns to hate, although many will tell you it does.*

If you truly loved your partner before the break up, you may become angry, but you will still love them.

> *If you heal correctly, eventually your love will shift from a state of "being in love" to one of simply loving the individual with no strings attached.*

You will be able to fall in love again.

> *When we open ourselves up to feel and express love, our capacity to love increases.*

The more you give the more you have to give. Unconditional love gives our partner freedom, and sometimes it means we have to let go and wish them happiness.

Once the shock has worn off, and you have moved through the grief process to the point of achieving acceptance of the circumstances, your next step is to forgive. The only way you can move forward is to forgive yourself, your partner, and anyone else involved in the situation. If necessary review forgiveness in Chapter Two.

It's common to experience low self esteem and fear about your future after a breakup. Your energy level will most likely be low, which makes it more arduous to think about, and plan for, an unknown future.

> *Due to low energy and lack of self-esteem it can be difficult for an individual to consider moving forward with his or her life and to put the past behind.*

This can become a period of stagnation, or what I like to call the "wallowing stage." The only way out is to forgive and to take each day as it comes.

Chapter One talked about eliminating expectation, so don't project your expectations into the future...live in the moment. Besides, if you are anything like me, when you are experiencing sadness your projections will tend to be all doom and gloom.

When you are ready to forgive, and move out of the "wallowing stage," you can do the release exercise in Chapter One. You will find that the heavy burden of heartache you were carrying around with you will become light.

When a loved one dies, or a serious illness afflicts you or someone close, how do you get through the crisis? First you will need to grieve and then when you are ready, forgive. With a death or illness, who do you forgive?

To facilitate your healing you may need to forgive God, yourself, the one who left, or the person responsible for your loss, maybe even the caregivers. Try to rise above your life and objectively consider your predicament.

> *There are two main perspectives from which you can view your situation.*

One perspective is to see your life as ruined, and feel that everything in the universe is working against you. You can adopt the attitude of hopelessness, give up, and remain in a state of stagnation.

On the other hand, you can draw upon your inner strength and gain wisdom from strife. You can discover the positive attributes within the situation, such as the time you were allotted with the loved one who passed away and how they impacted your life. If you were to lose the functioning of your legs due to an accident or illness there still remains a rainbow in the dark sky above. It is up to you to decide what the positive aspects of your particular situation are.

> *Remember that if one person can conceive an idea, accomplish an amazing feat, or overcome impossible obstacles to achieve joy, you can, too!*

Always keep your hope alive.

> *Hope and intend for a cure, for the pain to ease, for life to become easier, for the miracle to happen.*

Amazingly while writing this chapter of this book, I received news that threw me off balance for awhile. I learned that my aunt, "my second mom," was diagnosed with cancer. I wasn't going to share this experience with you but, I have been guided to do so. I am going to attempt to show you how I responded to this unsought, unexpected crisis delivered to my life. I feel it necessary to give you some background about me. Please stay with me and I will try not to digress for long.

Upon completing my own initial self analysis, I became aware that not only was it difficult for me to express my anger, it was doubly difficult for me to share my pain. I was the one to whom everyone turned for advice, a shoulder to cry on or just an ear to listen to them. It warmed my heart that I could help in some way. I realized that I denied my friends and family the opportunity to also feel good by helping me through my grief, my pain, and life's low points.

> *When faced with unpleasant situations I tend to retreat into myself.*

I never saw the value of sharing my gloomy emotions with others. I also probably never felt truly safe to share, due to my own insecurities.

In the last few years I have become better at sharing those emotions with others, especially with my husband Alex. The year 1998 brought an astronomical amount of change to my life. It took me months to work through the grief process and to redefine my being.

> *I knew that the changes were necessary for my growth and for me to fully align with my destined path.*

Knowing things are right and for the best does not make them easier to experience.

When my mom called to tell me her identical twin had cancer and the prognosis was poor, I felt like someone had punched me in the gut. A few tears fell during my conversation with my mom, but I made sure to comfort her and show her compassion. After I hung up, all I could think about was how the news impacted me, and that the whole thing "really sucked." When Alex arrived home I shared the news with him and he promptly held me so I could cry. I typically didn't allow myself to spend much time crying. Alex gave me space to brood as I retreated into myself.

> *I was conscious of my retreat and understood that this is how I figure things out, but I also knew that I needed to share my feelings with Alex.*

I am going to digress once more and share some of my history with you. It is important in order for you to understand my experience. I am an RN, so when my father and uncle, the two men I admired most in the world, chose to die at home, I became their nurse. I didn't know if I was strong enough to do this again with my aunt. I am honored to have been given the ability and the opportunity to care for these wonderful men. They taught me there is an "art" to dying with dignity.

> *The insight I gleaned from them never could have been absorbed through textbooks or from patients with whom I had no true emotional bond.*

When each man passed on, it was like witnessing the birth of a child.

> *I was in awe of their acceptance, and the energy of unconditional love that surrounded them during their final moments.*

I truly believe that life continues forever and that death is really a birth into a new life. Being the caregiver, I pushed aside my grief. I felt it was a luxury in which I couldn't afford to indulge.

My grief hit hard only after everything was taken care of. In the quiet, I realized that I would never see my dad or my uncle again. Their chapter in my life book was closed.

I reflected on these experiences as I tried to figure out how I was going to deal with my beloved aunt's illness. I was angry, despondent and hopeless all at the same time. My emotional body begged for release through tears but I allowed only a few to fall. My physical body quickly responded to the suppression of tears by creating a tension migraine. "I felt I deserved" the migraine because I give great advice to others, but was refusing to heed that same advice myself.

I knew that I had to talk to my aunt, so when she was released from the hospital I called her. She told me that she wasn't going to give up as she has everything in the world to live for. We both cried a little and laughed a lot. By chance Alex and I had a trip already planned which included a visit to my mom and aunt. Aunt Barb and I discussed the upcoming visit, which both of us were looking forward to. We expressed our love for each other then said good-bye.

> *When I hung up I took stock of the situation at a deeper level than before and finally I allowed my emotions to flow.*

I cried for me, Aunt Barb (who has had her share of pain in this life) and I cried for my mom (her identical twin). I then calmed down and reviewed the entire situation from an objective standpoint.

> *I saw that we are never given more than we can handle.*

I knew that my aunt would use her inner strength to cope and that her positive attitude would facilitate her recovery. I also understood that if the situation presented itself, there would be no question that I would nurse her as I had nursed my father and uncle.

I remembered all the times Aunt Barb has been there for me and all the fun we have shared. I am blessed to have been born into a family of strong, diverse, intelligent, humorous, loving, individuals.

Now with my refound power, I am going to focus on hope for a remission and enjoy the time that we are able to share...now.

This whole process took me approximately a week to work through. I grieved the change in my Aunt's health status, but I refuse to grieve over her demise before it happens.

> *I have reestablished my balance.*

I have come to peace with the situation because this terrible experience is preferable, to never having known the great woman who is my Aunt Barb.

> *Life is in constant motion.*

You can decide to move actively with it, creating a vibrant life for you to live, or you can decide to passively watch life go by and do only enough to exist. Notice I said exist, not live.

> *To experience life you have to be a creative participant,*
> *not a fearful and inactive bystander.*

Overcoming the obstacles on your path becomes your choice. As hard as it sometimes is to face, life does go on.

> *You can continue forward with it or lie down and waste*
> *the rest of your time here on earth.*

Again the choice is entirely up to you. We have full control over our responses to the twists and turns of the great game called life. Having this control gives you power and freedom over any and all situations. Know and embody this truth and always remember that you are loved. And with love, all things are possible.

5

FINDING BALANCE IN LIFE

The previous chapter discussed overcoming the huge obstacles life throws at you. In this chapter we will discuss an overview of stress and present various tools to assist you in living a balanced life.

Stress is a very popular word in our American culture.

> *Our society has created psychological and physiological illnesses as a result of our inability to cope with stress.*

The illnesses are very real but in my opinion unnecessary.

Today, Americans live a fast paced life, with fewer support systems than in the past. Our family structure has evolved to include many single parent families, and two-income families (due to necessity rather than preference) and many have moved away from their established support system.

> *The daily routines of job, child rearing and accomplishing the everyday tasks of life make it tough to find quiet time.*

We discusssed in Chapter One that most people do not delve into their essence.

> *This could be due to the difficulty of finding quiet time, or, that their quiet time is easily filled with activities, anything to eliminate going within to find their answers.*

Electronics provide individuals with the ability to create diversion and noise effortlessly. Many people fall into bed at night exhausted, only to awake feeling the same way.

> *We must learn how to quiet our environment and our minds, if we are ever to achieve a state of wellness.*

It is impossible to eliminate stress from our lives, nor would we desire to do so. We require a certain amount of stress to function.

> *When we push ourselves to the limit to accomplish an endeavor important to us it is exhilarating and it is also considered stressful. This would be labeled "good stress."*

Before we can change something we must first understand it, as pointed out in the first chapter.

What exactly is stress?

> *Stress is the state produced by a perceived challenge or threatening situation, while the change, or stimulus that evokes this state is, the stressor.*[3]

Response to stress is individual. What is stressful for one person may not be for another.

> *Stress becomes problematic when we feel unable to cope with the demands of life.*

Hans Selye first stated that: "Stress is essentially the rate of the wear and tear on the body."[4]

> *The inability to cope arises from an individual's perception that he or she has no control over a given situation.*

Therefore if we change our perceptions of stress, we will change our reactions and responses to it.

Your perceptions are created in the mental body, causing reactions to the stress that is felt by the emotional body, and your responses to stress are manifested in the physical body. Allow me to explain.

> *When a stressful event occurs, our mental body determines if it is harmful or beneficial to us.*

Our emotional body takes the information and elicits the correct emotion for us to experience such as fear, dread,

3 & 4 Brunner/Suddarth *"Textbook Medical-Surgical Nursing, fifth edition"* (1984 J.B. Lippincott)

horror, sadness, and even pride, joy, or relief. Our physical body is then responsible for creating action such as fleeing, crying, laughing. Do you understand?

> *Stress, good or bad, affects every aspect of our being every single day of our life.*

The ultimate goal of this chapter is to give you the means to take care of the stress in your spiritual, mental or emotional bodies before it can begin to manifest illness in your physical body.

> *Our physical bodies were created to respond to stress on a short term basis. It is called the "fight or flight response."*

Its purpose is to provide the body with the needed energy to either run from a situation or to stand our ground and fight. The diagram below shows the designed biological response and what the outcome can be if the response is sustained. As stated earlier, when we experience grief, sadness, anger and frustration, we need to feel these emotions fully but for a limited time only. Each situation is different and no one can tell you exactly how long is too long, but as a rule, frustration and anger should be expressed and released very quickly to reduce the risk of causing harm to yourself.

STRESS RESPONSE DIAGRAM

DESIGNED RESPONSE:	PURPOSE:	LONG TERM EFFECT:
Increased Heart Rate	Pumps Blood Faster	**High Blood Pressure**
Increased Breathing	Increased Oxygen Supply	**Chest Pain**
Digestion Stops, Blood Leaves the Head	Blood Diverts to the Large Muscles	**Migraine Headaches, Ulcers, Cold Hands and Feet**
Increased Blood Coagulation	Decreased Blood Loss Should Injury Occur	**Increased Chance of Blood Clots/Stroke**
Extra Sugars and Insulin Released into the Blood-Stream	Provide More Energy	**Tired Due to Low Blood Sugar**
Stress Messages are Sent to the Muscles[5]	Prepare Muscles for ActionPrepare Muscles for Action	**Fatigue**

[5] Stress Reduction Workshop, Career Track Boulder CO. 1992

Let's look at some common stressors. They include, but are not limited to: Death of a loved one, birth, divorce, promotions, demotions, serious arguments, vacations, lack of resources, worry, and meeting the demands of others, at home or in the office.

The work place, as you no doubt know, can be very stressful to one's life. For example, Corporate America has embraced the concept of "downsizing." "Downsizing" eliminates personnel and increases the workload for those left behind. It can provoke individuals to feel overworked, frustrated, unappreciated and insecure about their future with their employer.

> *Most of us are capable of dealing with the "big" things in life such as work, somehow it's the "little" things, piled on top of one another, that really throw us off balance.*

Living with sustained stress is unacceptable and just about everything can cause stress. So lets explore ways to find balance.

> *Our reactions and responses to stress are related to our perception of it*

Big, little, positive or negative, stressors have one of three traits associated with them. They are change, loss, and the feeling of helplessness in a situation. Depending on the individual and the situation, one may experience all three or just one of the stress associated traits. How do you switch your perspective about change, loss and lack of control? It's not easy and will require effort. BUT YOU'RE WORTH IT! Initially we will discuss feeling helpless and the perception that you have no control.

> *We tend to feel out of control when the circumstances surrounding us occur without our intent.*

Sometimes we will set something in motion that takes on a life of its own and we stand back thinking, "this is not what I had in mind." When this occurs all you can do is choose the best possible option available within the particular set of circumstances.

> *You may have no control over the situation, including its solution, but you have control of how you respond to the event.*

An example is a story that made the news. This particular account is derived from students who knew the participants. It is a perfect example of how our actions at times do not follow our intentions.

A group of college kids were "messing around" in the lounge of their dorm one night when, as a joke, one of them set a piece of paper on fire. Evidently thinking the fire was out, they left the lounge. Another student passing by saw the paper was still burning and extinguished it. Believe it or not, it still wasn't put out completely and the dorm burned. Aside from the property damage, one student was seriously injured. The student who started the fire was prosecuted for arson.

> *I am not judging the right or wrong of the incident but pointing out that the result was not the student's beginning intention.*

I would surmise that the student incurred a stress reaction due to a feeling of loss of control over the given situation. The student did lose control over the situation, but wishing things were different would be a waste of time and energy.

> *Many people focus their energy on things they cannot change, which reinforces their feeling of helplessness.*

Instead they should keep their focus in the present and make positive choices that will assist them in dealing with the crisis.

> *The past cannot be undone, but choices for how to deal with the predicament are available.*

The above case demonstrates to us that every action counts and we sometimes entangle ourselves in situations that are unpleasant.

> *The best way to gain control over a situation is to rise above it and become an observer, instead of a participant.*

This allows you to be objective and clears away the emo-

tional ties you have attached to the situation. You still hold
the responsibility for your role in creating the situation.

> *When you view your life objectively, you are able to make
> rational decisions about what to do next.*

As stated before, there are always choices to be made,
but you must elect to do so.

> *When we sit back pondering why life is the way it is and
> refuse to make a decision as to what action to pursue, life
> will decide for us.*

When life chooses the solution for us, often it is not to
our liking. When you think that everything is out of control,
sit back, take a deep breath, view your predicament objec-
tively, choose a rational and appropriate action, then act.
Hindsight is 20/20, so don't beat yourself up over the past.

> *Learn from the experience, release your judgment about
> it, and go on with your life because life, does and always
> will continue to move forward with or without you.*

We will now look at how to cope with change and loss.
The previous chapter explains that when you experience
change you also experience loss.

> Our mind fears change of any kind.

People will complain that their life is boring and that they are in a "rut." When you are in a "rut" it is because you do the same thing every day out of habit and it feels comfortable, but boring. Many individuals have their life on a planned schedule and they will not deviate from that schedule. If something throws their schedule off panic sets in and they find it difficult to cope. I am talking about the little things that can throw a schedule off such as unexpected company, waking up late for work, the car breaking down, your child becoming sick, etc.

> If the little things blow a person out of the water, how can he or she expect to handle the bigger, life altering, changes?

Nature teaches us that everything changes. Day to night, fall to winter, young to old...it's a fact of life.

> No matter what the change is, you can always find the positive aspect, or you can choose to dwell on the negative aspect of it.

The way to deal with change is to embrace the unknown and go with the flow. As discussed earlier, living in the present moment assists you in flowing with life.

> Viewing your life optimistically will enable you to see that things in life have a way of working themselves out.

Everything has a reason for occurring, and it is not always necessary for us to know why. Accept the circumstances, be brave and make new choices.

I know people who are miserable in their marriage. They will not leave it because they know what to expect from their current partner, even if the relationship consists of arguing, cold wars and discontentment. The unknown of being alone or finding a new relationship is more threatening and awakens fear in them, so they stay where they are.

> *When you are faced with life's changes and/or loss it is the perfect time to reflect on your life and decide how you will live the rest of it.*

The introduction of this book touched on how you are the co-creator of your life. Let me explain this in further detail.

We bring everything to us with God's help. This is a difficult concept to assimilate, as most of us would rather not take responsibility for the pain and sorrow that occurs in our life. In chapter one you identified your attributes, the good, the bad and the ugly. You then released the ones that no longer served you, but you first needed to distinguish why the attribute was a part of you. Determining why the attribute existed was vitally important as you could not release it until you accepted the energy surrounding it. This means that you took responsibility for the creation of the attribute.

I am not implying that people consciously create everything bad in their lives. Heck, most people don't consciously create the good in their lives.

> *Your Soul creates and designs situations that are meant to lead you closer to God, and sometimes the situations are not very pleasant.*

If you look at your life and dissect it, you will find that you played a part in everything that has happened to you. Keep in mind that when a loved one becomes ill or dies you did not create their death or illness. However, you helped create the bond between the two of you so that together you could share the experience.

> *When you take responsibility for your life this powerfully, you can make your world be whatever you want it to be.*

Losing your job may be viewed as the best or worst thing that ever happened to you. Instead of looking for someone to blame and whining how unfair life is, examine your situation, seek the positive and explore why this was created for you by you. There may be another job in which you will be happier and more fulfilled.

> *Understand that nothing is ever truly lost, and that some experiences are meant to be stepping stones to other experiences.*

When one door closes another always opens. Instead of seeing things as lost, be of the mind that it was time to move on and the Universe acted with you to create the opportunity for it to happen.

> *Coping with change becomes easier when you seek the positive aspects of the situation and understand if and how you were the co-creator.*

If you find that you were the co-creator and you disliked the predicament, then create a different scenario the next time around.

> *Sometimes we create stress for ourselves through self sabotage.*

A relationship or job is going great and for whatever reason we engage in a self-defeating behavior that fouls everything up. The behavior itself is important as is the result. You created a behavior that caused an adverse outcome.

> *This is why I keep repeating that you must take responsibility for every aspect of your life or you are destined to repeat the same behaviors and mistakes over and over again.*

Are you still skeptical as to your role in the events of your life? Let me try this example in an attempt to show you what I mean.

Most of us know first or second hand a person who appears to be on the path of self-destruction. You look at this person and clearly see how they are creating their own downfall. Their problems could be anything, such as the inability to hold a job, being addicted to drugs, failed relationships, loss of money through poor decisions or overindulgence of the self. When you discuss this person with others, and you know you do, you say things like, if only he would do this or that, things would be better. If she can't see that she is ruining her life she must be blind. Maybe he is your friend and you take him aside and tell him, "If you don't start showing up on time you're going to get fired." The very next day he arrives late again and you shake your head and say "What's the matter with you? Can't you see that you're throwing your job away with your actions? Don't you even care?" As time goes on and the same things happen repeatedly, you give up trying to help.

> *You then say something like "he has to hit rock bottom before he will wake up."*

My question to you is, do you choose to continue living your life blindly? Do you choose to stay asleep or are you going to wake up and consciously co-create a life filled with joy and happiness? HELLO! I am talking to you! If you can see how someone else is responsible for his or her life situation or crisis, can you not see that you are also responsible for yours?

Back to coping with change and loss. When change occurs analyze your new options.

> *Think of it as a challenge and not a problem.*

Again you may not be able to alter the situation, but you can choose how you will respond internally to what life is dishing out.

> *This gives you total control and empowers you in every situation.*

It also reduces your stress response because you realize that you do have choices and are not helpless.

Another great exercise is to examine all of the possible consequences of all the possible options that could arise from a single situation. Write the list out, then study it to determine what the worst thing that could happen is. When you do this, often you will find that the truly worst thing that could happen is far less than what you imagined. Next, ask yourself if you can cope and live with the worst possible outcome. Take the scenario through to the end by actually figuring out what you would do if the worst outcome occurred. Maybe the worst thing is being fired. What would you do? Perhaps you would collect unemployment or you would find a different job. Maybe to find another job you would need to relocate, so you would do everything you would need to make it happen.

> *The answers to all of your questions are available to you from you. All you need to do is calm your mind and listen to your heart.*

Once you decide that you can cope with the worst possible scenario, you need to work out the best possible scenario. This is the one that you will want to focus all of your energy into because you never want to dwell on negative outcomes, as it may empower them and cause them to happen. You did the worst case scenario exercise to show yourself that you were able to deal with the worst scenario if it came to pass. This exercise also assists you in uncovering and eliminating your fears.

> *Sometimes we do not listen to our inner guidance because we don't like the solution or are afraid of it.*

Here is an example of how I dealt with what I saw as a disaster. My second husband requested a separation. We lived three hours from my friends and family and he didn't want to leave our house or the area he worked in. The only solution was for the kids and me to move back to my home town where, thanks to the Universe, I found a job.

The kids and I were very upset and we really wanted the marriage to work out. I gave my husband a five month deadline in which a decision for our future had to be made. I scrutinized all of the available options and their consequences. I chose to cope by helping my children cope and immersing myself in my new job. I told the kids that we had little power over their step dad's decision, so there was no point in us worrying about it.

> *This gave us the power to make the situation what we wanted it to be.*

We decided to have fun and imagined that we were on a city safari and that a great adventure was waiting to happen. I attempted to make every day new for them and the by-product was that my days were also new. The time apart was definitely not all rosy, but we did survive and we were able to have some enjoyment.

> *I was not on my path consciously, but something inside told me to take each day as it came. So I did.*

My point is that we are capable of living with bad situations, we just need to find a new perspective. I took what I felt at the time to be one of the worst situations and tried to see the positive side of it. Trust me when I say that I really had to search for it, but I did find positive reasons for our separation. Here are three of them: First my mother was a new widow and being in the area allowed me to spend time with her as she became acclimated to her new life. Secondly, hindsight being 20/20, this time allowed me to look back and realize that my new job not only brought me life long friends, it gave me the experience I would need for my future jobs. The third reason was that I became stronger and it was the true beginning of the development of my relationship with myself.

> *"God does not give us more than we can bear," is a quaint or trite saying depending on your view, but nevertheless it is true.*

History teaches us that we humans are a sturdy and resilient group of beings.

Another easy way to eliminate stress is to ask yourself if whatever is causing you the stress will matter in the future. Be honest, will the fact that you're late for work or that some task didn't get accomplished, impact you one year down the line? Will it matter in fifty years, seventy-five, or even in one hundred years?

This question puts life events that we expand into trauma into a clear perspective. If your house fails to get cleaned, trust me it will be waiting for you when you have time to get to it. Your partner forgot to pick up milk on their way home, guess what...you will all be okay without it for a day.

> *Individuals will argue over the littlest and stupidest things that in the grand scheme of life really do not, and will not, ever matter.*

There is already enough misery in the world, so why do we insist on creating more?

> *You have the power, use it to create harmony in your life and in the world.*

There are numerous books and articles written on ways to deal with stress and I recommend reading any one of them if you feel you need additional help in reducing your stress level.

> *The "fight or flight" response creates an excess of energy within and if you are not going to flee or do physical combat it must be utilized.*

Your goal should be to use the energy in a constructive manner. When I am in a stressful situation (such as writing this chapter!), I walk away and focus my energy on something else for awhile. Then I am able to return and refocus on the situation because I am more relaxed and my mind is clearer.

> To move through your stress and expend the excess energy there are a variety of things you can do.

You can clean your house, discuss the predicament with a friend, go for a walk, meditate, exercise, laugh, relax in a warm bath, and the list goes on and on. There is no need to go into detail about these activities except to discuss humor.

> Humor is said to be the only thing that comes unchanged to us directly from the Universe.

I have read many spiritual books that tell us we can never truly understand the magnificence of God from our earthly perspective, but we can glimpse it through humor. Researchers are finding that laughter actually increases our bodies' immune response. The movie "Patch Adams" is about a physician who believes in using humor to heal. Often people crack jokes to break tense moments. I have cried my most intense tears and laughed my heartiest laugh at the funerals of my friends and family.

> Laughter is contagious and a wonderful release.

Here is another cliché: "Laugh and the world laughs with you, cry and you cry alone." Most of us take life far too seriously. I have learned to laugh at myself, mainly because if I didn't I probably would have cried. Comics use real life occurrences for their material and people laugh.

> *Laughter is a wonderful way to ease stress and it is healthy for you. My advice is to laugh as often as you can.*

Stress is inevitable so you must develop the skills necessary to cope with it. A prolonged stress response will eventually cause your physical body to fail. Stress is a physical message designed to tell you that you are not aligned with your Soul's path. You are the co-creator of your life. There are always options available to you in any situation. You must become objective, seek the positive, flow with life, laugh, take action and know that you do have the courage and tools within you to transcend any situation that comes your way.

6

TRUE LIFE APPLICATIONS

*T*his chapter is composed of real life stories about normal people who have applied the truths contained in this book to their life. The stories are written in the third person as they told it to me.

> *The intent of this chapter is to demonstrate how others have overcome obstacles and/or how the Universe has worked in their lives.*

I hope you are able to glean some inspiration from their lessons and triumphs.

Stan

Our first story is about Stan and the multiple lessons he learned and the growth he acquired from committing an act of theft. It proves there is something positive in everything.

Stan came from a good home and was raised to know the difference between right and wrong. One of his bigger life lessons had to do with money. Stan viewed money as something which he never had enough of and a part of him resented having to work when some of his friends didn't.

Instead of starting college right after high school, Stan chose to remain at home, work and save money for the winter semester. Stan's boss gave him additional responsibilities and often left him alone at work. Stan felt that he was not saving enough money and needed more, so he opted to steal from his employer.

Stan didn't take large amounts of money but he did take it more than once. Simultaneously he began to experience unusual expenses. His car broke down on more than one occasion, and he began losing or misplacing his money. Eventually Stan was caught stealing at work and was prosecuted. He was embarrassed, spent time in jail, and was ordered to pay restitution plus fines that amounted to more than he took. He knew that what he did was wrong and he apologized for it, but he still needed to learn a few things.

Stan became angry at the world for what he saw as unjust punishment. He spent many hours alone and with guidance, he took the opportunity to look inside himself.

> *He learned that if you break a universal law the universe will acknowledge your action.*

Lovingly, It will not let you off the hook, even if no one else on the planet knows what you have done. Stan stole from his employer, so the Universe took from him by creating instances in which he would need to spend that money, such as car repairs. Stan also learned that he was the sole creator of his plight and he needed to take full responsibility for it.

> *Once he embraced responsibility and quit being a victim, his next step was to forgive.*

Stan forgave himself for betraying the trust of his boss and for the actual theft. However, he found it difficult to forgive his boss for prosecuting him and he couldn't let go of his anger. This aspect of Stan's overall lesson took the longest to reach fruition. Stan finally reached the point where he was able to forgive his boss and release his anger.

> *When he finally accomplished this feat he found a sense of peace and true freedom within himself.*

The last part of his lesson is one that many should learn. The importance Stan placed upon money caused him to give his power over to it. Money was more valued than trust, honesty and the law.

> *Stan came to understand that money is nothing more than a tool to be used, not a deity to be worshipped.*

He realized that he was not happier when he had money compared to when he didn't. Money allowed Stan to do more things but ultimately his attachment to it cost him his physical freedom.

> *Stan's punishment appeared to be excessive but upon review he needed the harshness in order to complete the lesson quickly.*

Stan also maintains that the universe may have slapped him but it was a gentle slap. He knows that the lesson could have been presented more forcefully. Stan has his life back on track and is doing wonderfully.

Tina

> *This is Tina's story about how the universe created a miracle in her life.*

Tina is a retired nurse and has pursued her spiritual growth. Tina became a Reiki Master and shares her gift with anyone who is in need of a healing touch. In the late seventies, Tina began to experience hearing loss. She did everything possible to fix the problem except to obtain a hearing aid. Tina remembered her mother's experience with hearing loss, and how she spent much money and false hope on hearing aids that always failed. In 1997 Tina found a hearing aid that cost one hundred and fifty dollars, so she purchased it. The device worked well. Tina still had difficulty following conversations, especially if the speaker wasn't facing her, but her hearing was better with the aid than without it. Tina also did energy work (Reiki) on herself regularly to heal her hearing loss.

Between Christmas and New Years eve of 1998 Tina was having coffee with her niece when she experienced a popping in her ear. To her amazement her hearing was restored to approximately ninety percent.

> *Tina no longer requires a hearing aid and is delighted with her gift from God, Goddess, All That Is.*

My Story

> *This story confirms that God and Goddess do give us what we ask for when we are sincere and it is for our best and highest good.*

I knew that I wanted a partner that I could grow and share my life with. I was having a difficult time finding the right man. I was also hesitant, because I knew without a doubt that I did not care to experience heartache again. One Sunday night I was meditating and told God and Goddess of my request for a life partner. I gave the "can't live without" parameters that my partner must possess, but left everything else up to the Universe, as I did not want to limit the limitless. Within thirty minutes Alex called and invited me to play volleyball that night with him. I declined as I had already made other plans! I had known Alex for a few years, we played co-ed adult volleyball together at our local school.

The week went by and it was a particularly tough one for me. By Thursday I was frustrated so when I arrived home from work, I meditated. I was feeling sorry for myself and told God and Goddess that they must not have been listening to me on Sunday. I repeated my request again just to be sure they heard and understood my needs. Within twenty minutes Alex called to invite me out to dinner and a movie any time over the weekend. Again, I declined, because I again had other plans. We talked for awhile and after we hung up the light bulb went on. I felt sheepish and stupid that my prayer was being answered not once but twice and I was too busy. Immediately I called Alex back and asked him if his offer was still open. He said yes, so we made a date for Friday night. We had a great time, and we seemed to click. Our next date was the following Sunday where he met my friends. After our Sunday date, you could say we became an item. We were dating for two months and two days when Alex asked me to marry him. We were wed two months later in an outdoor ceremony at my house (ours now). Our friends and family surrounded us, and the service was performed by a friend of ours. It was a storybook wedding. Alex and I cried tears of joy. It seemed that he and I were encircled by our love for each other and the love of God and Goddess, our friends, family, and children. As of this writing we have been married for nineteen blissful months.

> *So you see happy endings can and do happen!*

Jane and Dick

This story is about Jane and the lesson she learned about unconditional love of self and others.

Jane dated Dick for three years. Jane enjoyed fun, friends and family. She was a vibrant, energetic, and outgoing individual. Dick was more on the serious side and he liked to spend time alone with Jane. You could describe Dick as analytical and opinionated. Their relationship went smoothly for the first six months, but then Dick tried to impose his will upon Jane. Jane felt that she loved Dick, so she wanted to do what ever she needed to do to make him happy. They fought about how Jane was not living up to Dick's expectations. Their relationship was on a roller coaster, with highs and lows, no in-between.

They became engaged and moved in together. Dick continued to express his dissatisfaction with Jane. At least he told her what she needed to change to please him. Jane made the changes and gave up the things in life that pleased her, but it was never enough. Dick continued to add to the list. He sought total control over Jane, from what she wore, to what she thought, to whom she associated with.

As time went on, Jane's friends told her that she wasn't the same person they loved and adored. They also expressed to her that the changes were not for the better.

> *Jane became depressed, sad, and was in a state of confusion most of the time. Their relationship became an on-again, off-again experience, depending on the day.*

Jane sought counsel and her lesson was clearly defined for her. First, Jane failed to love herself unconditionally.

> *She changed her core being to please another, which is never the correct thing to do.*

Second, Jane was willing to stay in a relationship that caused her pain, because she was afraid to venture into the unknown.

> It was vital for Jane to examine who she was and what
> she desired from life.

This took her awhile to contemplate.

Jane remained with Dick as she strived to find the woman she had left behind. Dick became even more controlling and the final straw was his refusal to allow Jane to spend time with her own family and most of her friends. Jane finally realized that she was a very nice person, and the original real Jane didn't need fixing. Gathering her courage she ended the relationship. She mourned the loss, and started a new life—one she controlled for herself. Jane learned that unconditional love of self and others is the foundation to all relationships.

> Jane will never alter her core being for another again,
> nor will she ever ask it of another.

She has forgiven herself and Dick and realizes they came together to teach one another a basic truth called unconditional love.

Marie

Here is Marie's story which is about following your inner guidance.

> Marie had set out to discover her soul's path for this
> lifetime.

She had a good job that she liked and excelled at.

The further her growth in consciousness took her the more aware she became that she would need to leave her job. This brought up many fears, such as how she would pay her bills and support her family. Marie continued to expand her awareness and began to feel restless.

> *She was certain that her soul had a plan for how to live the rest of her life but she was clueless as to what it was.*

Work became chaotic for Marie, which carried over into her home life. It was a struggle for her to go to work everyday, let alone to enjoy it. It seemed to Marie that she was expending a lot of energy trying to stay in her comfort zone. She had traversed enough lessons to know that following her soul's path was inevitable.

> *Marie's inner guidance told her that she would be embarking on her new path shortly, so she watched for the opportunity to present itself.*

Marie's work environment deteriorated even more, to the point that she began to welcome a change without fear. She asked the Universe to show her the opportunity and to make her abundantly aware when it arrived. When she least expected it, the opportunity presented itself. Marie and her boss could no longer get along and it appeared to her that her boss was setting her up to fail. One day Marie's boss blew a situation out of proportion and blamed her for it. Marie was upset but she easily recognized the incident for what it was. Amazingly, Marie not only knew it was time to leave her job but also perceived what her soul work would entail. On pure faith Marie left her employment, allowing the universe to work the details out. Marie was honored by her employer for her years of excellent service, and she was given severance pay. Everything had been orchestrated perfectly. Marie aligned with her true destiny, and the Universe provided her with the means to meet all of her needs.

Karen

This story exemplifies how the universe will bless us when we least expect it.

Karen is a college student who lives away from home and works to pay for her expenses. She is self aware and endeavors to raise her consciousness. Karen applied herself in high school and hoped to obtain a scholarship for college. She was angry and disappointed when she didn't get one.

> *Karen got over her anger and disappointment quickly and went on with her life.*

She applied herself and achieved excellent grades her first semester of college.

Work and school were going fine, but nevertheless Karen began to feel down. She saw that many of her friends were planning to go away for spring break and she couldn't afford to go anywhere herself.

> *Karen started complaining that her friends had something she didn't.*

Deep down, she didn't begrudge the fact that her friends received grants or scholarships, or that their parents were able to give them money. She was just bemoaning her circumstances.

> *When everything appeared to be the darkest, Karen received a letter informing her that she was the recipient of a scholarship.*

The money was for her current semester, that had already been paid for, so it could be applied to her next year's tuition. Karen was immediately grateful to her benefactor and to the universe for the unexpected gift. She was also humbled. She realized that complaining gets you nowhere and that we are not always aware of the treasures life holds for us just around the corner.

No Agendas!

This story was submitted to me by a friend and I have chosen to include it as written. Here is her touching story.

Eighteen years ago, one year into "the relationship of my life," all my training and all my programming kicked in...I wanted to get married. It didn't matter that he told me from day one that marriage was not an option.

> *Somehow he had managed to mature into an understanding of relationship as "unconditional love without agendas."*

I still had the marriage agenda in spades. So we broke up. What a horrible conversation! Two people, feeling pure love, but unable to find a way to align our paths...It was emotional, painful and absolutely inevitable.

Two weeks later I was still grieving over the loss that I had created. I finally looked at what was essential to my happiness within this relationship and discovered that the only essential was his happiness. I finally realized that by dropping my agenda (marriage) I could have and enjoy "the love of my life."

> *I realized that creative and honest communication could open the door to a level of relationship that I had never dreamed of before.*

So I asked God and Goddess All That Is, for a second chance and a sign.

The next morning I went to work. I was sitting at my desk working at my computer when he walked in. "I have some window screens from your house in my car," he said. His voice was low and full of emotion, his eyes sad. "I had taken them to my house for repairs. I'm just going to put them in your car."

> *My heart skipped a beat—hope was being reborn!*

I offered to help him move the screens between cars and he accepted.

Now, my friend was an airline pilot who flew out of the large commercial airports in New York City. I was a computer consultant and traveled often with my business. As we worked he asked if I had any business trips coming up. "Actually," I answered, "I'll be flying to Chicago on Friday." "Oh...what airport are you flying from?"

"Hartford," I answered. (Not his.)
"What airline?"
"United." (His.)
"What time?" he asked.
"Nine A.M." I said.

At this point he put the screens in his hands down, looked me straight in the eyes, took a breath and added, "Now would you care to guess who the pilot is who is flying you to Chicago?" We spent the weekend together in Chicago, walking and talking, listening and learning. We are still together today.

> *No, we're not married...we don't even live in the same state!*

But we are unconditionally, unselfishly in love and best friends as well. Amazing what can happen when our personal agendas get out of the way!

Katie

This story is about Katie who used the love from God and Goddess, and the love within herself, to heal a chronic illness.

Katie was diagnosed with fibromyalgia approximately six years ago. Fibromyalgia is a chronic illness with a variety of symptoms. It was normal for Katie to awaken with a headache, muscle stiffness, fatigue, and generalized body aches. She would consider this a "good" day. Katie's "bad" days were when she experienced either migraine headaches or severe muscle spasms that kept her in bed.

> *With great effort she was able to work and care for her family but her quality of life was diminishing.*

Katie became interested in alternative healing because modern medicine was barely able to keep her pain at a tolerable level. She went to a local Reiki practitioner for a healing session. When the session was completed she felt better and decided to become a Reiki Master herself.

> *Katie continued to experience pain, and her headaches would become so intense that she would actually wish she was dead —anything to stop the pain that racked her body.*

Katie was on her spiritual path and as she progressed she began to understand that it is possible to have miraculous healing. All you need is pure faith and unconditional love. She attempted to heal through God and usually received positive results although the results never stuck. Never giving up and continuing her spiritual growth, Katie embraced wellness for herself.

> *The missing factor to her being healed was herself.*

Katie visualized herself surrounded by white and golden light that originated from God, and then she took the light into her body to heal all that needed to be healed. She released everything within her that contained fear-based energy.

> *She had to take part in her healing and be responsible for her own wellness.*

Katie has been off her medication for awhile now and feels great. She experiences minor aches and pains that are usually relieved with aspirin. Katie's quality of life has improved immensely and she believes that she has been healed by the love inside he, r and the love generated to the world from God.

I would like to reiterate that the above stories are about real, everyday, people.

> *It doesn't take wealth or knowledge to apply the universal basic truths to your life.*

All it takes is dedication to self growth and persever-ance. This chapter illustrates the truth that joy, peace and unconditional love are for everyone who resides on this planet!

7

POSSIBILITIES

> *I love what the word possibility represents: potential,*
> *feasibility, what may be.*

The American dream that anyone can be anything is founded on the premise that all things are possible. Achieving the American dream is a desire that people around the globe share. Individuals from other countries leave all they are familiar with to immigrate here, just to pursue this dream. So the question is: why does the dream of prosperity, security and happiness elude so many?

> *I have personally sought the dream in my own way.*

I wanted a loving family and a nice home, and I wished to help people become healthy, which is why I became a nurse. By the time I was 34, I had two beautiful children, two divorces, a well paying, high stress nursing administrative job at a rural hospital and I was in a relationship that could best be described as tenuous.

> *I wasn't satisfied with my life because something remained missing.*

I thought maybe having a solid loving relationship with a man was the missing link but now I know that was not the case. It seemed that the harder I tried to achieve fulfillment, which to me was having it all, the more elusive it became, which prompted me to strive harder, which created more dissatisfaction and so the viscous cycle continued. What was wrong? Was it that I was looking for something that didn't exist? Were my goals and ideals only attainable in a dream state and if so then was this all life had to offer me?

> *I knew that finding the answers to these questions was paramount to my life, so I gave them much thought and I queried my friends, family and colleagues for their opinions on the subject.*

Answers were not forthcoming. Finally in frustration and anger I asked God if this was it. As described in the introduction of this book, it was at this point that I began to awaken spiritually. In this chapter I intend to illustrate for you the factors that I believe limit an individual's ability to attain all that is possible for him and to give you the tools so that you may open yourself up to the realm of possibilities.

Reason #1

> *The most important reason that individuals fail to achieve the American dream is that they never took the time to define what the concept of the dream means to them, or they focus their energy on one aspect of it such as prosperity (meaning money).*

To reach total fulfillment one must pursuit endeavors that encompass and satisfy their whole being. When asked what would create happiness for them people will answer: a good job, money, and a stable family life. Sounds good, but what does it mean? When questioned further most individuals cannot answer how they will accomplish their objectives. In reality, are all rich people happy, and poor people sad? How about the people who have stable jobs or careers or the ones who have a great home life, are they all happy? I believe the answer is no, because if it were true I wouldn't need to write this chapter. Okay, I know what you're thinking, what about the individuals who seem to have it all, great job, loving family life and tons of money, they must be happy, right? Again, the answer is most likely no, as evidenced by the top business people, elected officials, actors and athletes who have a job they love and plenty of money yet they appear in the news, time and time again because they were caught with drugs, getting divorced, having an affair, or doing something outrageous to erase their boredom.

We discussed earlier in this book that

> *happiness is something that must come from inside yourself and you must know what you are looking for in order to recognize it when it appears in your life.*

The definition of happiness, fulfillment, pleasure and joy is different for everyone. You need to take the time to find what your definition is and you need to include all the areas of your life. Ask yourself what would make you rise each morning with a smile on you face and close each night with a prayer of gratitude and thanks to God, Goddess, All That Is on your lips. Your desires can be big or small but they must be clearly defined.

> *Remember that you are a physical, mental, emotional, and spiritual being so be sure to include all of these aspects when you are determining your definition for happiness.*

> *Once you know what you are truly trying to achieve you will also know what you need to avoid and that leaves you more time and energy to devote to your dream.*

Specific goals are important not only as a focal point for you but they also help you to eliminate the things in your life that are not congruent with your dream.

Your dream should also be realistic, otherwise you are wasting precious time and energy and are doomed to fail. I am not talking about limitation, which we will get to later.

What I am trying to say is that you should not put energy in to something that will never be.

> *Instead you need to channel your resources into a dream that can be made possible.*

For example, My dream is to become a writer and teacher which opens the door to many possibilities and it is a dream that I can bring into fruition. But if I decided that I wanted to become a famous singer no amount of practice or hard work would bring that particular dream to life because I am not gifted in the music area. On this point of fact you have to take my word for it. Another example would be if you decided that you wanted to be married to a movie star. Although it could happen, this would not be a realistic goal for most individuals. Your dream would be more realistic if you identified the characteristics of the individual with whom you wish to marry and left specific names out entirely.

> *Being practical does not limit your possibilities, instead it channels your talents and desires into areas that are attainable for you and creates new possibilities that you may have never even thought of.*

Examine your life and determine in depth what it is that you need in order to be fulfilled, happy and joyful. Write everything down because there are more things possible in this world than most of us allow ourselves to think.

Reason #2

Limitation is reason number two. Limitation and conditioning were touched upon in Chapter Two. I ask you to stay with me here because the information warrants repeating.

> *I will attempt to relay the data differently so that you can fully comprehend the significance of the two concepts and not become bored.*

> *Limitation is a mental form of blindness to possibilities.*

The sun rises and then it sets every single day without thought, and that is how most individuals run their lives. They settle themselves into routines that are safe but those very same routines create a feeling of dissatisfaction and a longing for something different from life.

> *When the blinders of limitation are worn, regret is soon to be born.*

Let me explain what I mean by this rhyme. When you decide that you cannot do something with your child, or that you can't go on an outing with your friends because you haven't the time, you have limited yourself and chances are you will regret that you didn't find the time. Lack of time is only a perception.

> *When you have a clear realistic goal to aim for, you must then eliminate limitation or you will never achieve it.*

Time is only one example of how we limit ourselves. Individuals settle for an unfulfilled life because they do not see any other way of living. They view their life as unfulfilled because there is something missing such as enough money, correct timing, desire, or even the energy to put into a different way of being. They lack the understanding of how to bring their dream into fruition, so they become apathetic and they settle for less.

> *We are all masters at creating limitation in our lives and believe it or not, you are the one who creates the limitation that you experience.*

We are conditioned from early childhood by our family, religions, and society to be limited by the boundaries and the rules they make and expect us to adhere to.

> *The great people of our time transcended the boundaries set forth for them.*

They include but are not limited to Jesus, Buddha, Mother Theresa, Einstein, Plato, the Wright brothers, Princess Diana, Henry Ford and so many more.

> *God is limitless and we are all part of God so how can the limitless become limited?*

It's not possible except by our own making.

Limited thinking begins with phrases such as "if only," "but," and "I can't."

> *The only way to eliminate limitation is to think outside the box and to know in your heart that if you truly desire something, nothing can keep you from it but yourself.*

You can transcend your conditioning just like the great individuals listed above. In order to do this you must begin to think and behave in a manner that is unique to you. What does this mean? You will need to tear down all the preconceived ideas you have about anything and construct ideas that are your very own. This is difficult because it means that you must think for yourself and not be swayed by your family, church, friends, government, employer, role models or even teachers. It is like learning all over again.

> *In the end you may very well arrive at a way of thinking that is exactly, or very close to, what you were conditioned to believe but why you believe what you do will be based on your own reasons not someone else's.*

You must develop your own intrinsic value and belief system that you live by.

> *Our values and beliefs become the filter through which we view and interpret the events that occur around us.*

Conditioning tells us what to believe but the reasons are never personal so the belief never becomes a knowing. When you take the time to figure out why you believe a particular way, you have embodied the concept, and then it is just a matter of living your belief system.

> *When you break the shackles of conditioning and limitation you open a whole new world filled with endless possibilities for you to explore.*

Reason #3

The third reason individuals fail to achieve the American Dream is fear.

> *People fear many things such as change, failure, being different from others, loneliness, abandonment, commitment and the list goes on.*

As previously stated fear is created by the mind in order to keep you immobile. How do you overcome fear? This is a very good question.

> *You must confront your fears head on and by doing so you take away the power that the fear held you with.*

In order to confront your fear you first need to identify that it even exists. Next you need to establish why you have a particular fear, and then you can work on healing it.

Let's say you fear commitment. Now you need to understand why this fear developed.

> *It could be as simple as not wanting your freedom impinged upon or as complex as being hurt or abandoned in the past by individuals you loved.*

Only you can answer the question "Why" and you may need outside assistance to help you.

> *Fear is limiting so it has to be eradicated before you can truly eliminate limitation.*

"If you never try something you will never fail" the saying goes but, the question you have to ask yourself is "If you never try are you living your life to its fullest potential?"

> *Fear enhances our weaknesses such as self-doubt, low self-esteem, and the feeling of helplessness, and destroys many opportunities for fulfillment and joy.*

When you redefined your belief system you broke the

shackles of conditioning.

> *Many of our fears are programmed in us by others.*

If you grew up in a family where it was the norm that parents fight and argue, you may decide not to have a close significant other relationship. Your reasoning would be that you do not want to turn out just like your parents. This is programmed or conditioned thinking.

> *If you confront your fear then you can heal it by understanding that you are not your parents and thus you can be in an intimate loving relationship with another that does not include fighting and arguing.*

Here's another thing to think about. If your worst fear came true, would your life be enhanced because you pursued your goal even though your fear became a reality or would it be better for you to live your life "status quo" because of the possibility that your fear could materialize? You and only you can answer this question.

My brother dreamed of running his own restaurant but he had to first push aside his fear of failure, which he did. The restaurant failed, causing him to lose everything he had gained monetarily up to that point, but he will tell you that it was worth the risk because he knew that it was better to follow his dream than live the rest of his life regretting what might have been.

> Fear has been used throughout the ages by leaders to suppress the population.

When you give into fear you quash your own personal possibilities for this lifetime.

> There is a difference between being cautious and being fearful.

A person being cautious remains open to new opportunities and examines every angle to ensure their safety. A fearful person refuses to listen or see the new opportunities and they shut down all incoming information, thus sealing themselves off from the world.

> Fear can be powerful, but anyone wishing to can overcome it, just by facing it.

What fears do you hold on to that keep you from growing and living your dream?

Reason #4

> Distortion of the American Dream is the final reason many are unable to attain it.

It is my firm belief that our forefathers intended for the

American Dream to be intrinsic, rather than what it has become, which is extrinsic.

> *In other words the prosperity, security and pursuit of happiness would come from inner personal growth and not from outside of the individual in the form of wealth, status and power.*

The majority of Americans spend their time chasing money. They define success by how much they are worth financially, their job title, how big their house is and the things they are able to accumulate. There is a saying that goes "He who has the most toys when he dies is the winner."

> *When an individual bases his happiness on things outside himself he is never truly content.*

Once the newness wears off the thrill of owning something becomes blase`, and thus they need to go out and buy more stuff that they really do not need.

> *It is time for people to understand that the development of the self into a loving, compassionate, non-judgmental individual is the only way to find peace, joy, and happiness.*

By distorting the American Dream most have given up a very important aspect of it, which is freedom. The American way is to pursue money as stated earlier.

> *When you value something so much that you will do most anything for it, you become its slave.*

Individuals complicate their lives by acquiring objects they can't afford and probably do not need, and by seeking status through enrolling their children in all kinds of extracurricular activities such as sports and dance, and joining country clubs, etc. This requires them to work at jobs they do not necessarily like or that take up the majority of their time. I am not implying that people shouldn't work, what I am saying is that our priorities are messed up.

> *Men and women put so much effort into the making of money that they have little to no energy left to spend time alone or with their mates, children or extended families.*

Our society has developed into one in which the world of business dominates.

> *The upper echelon makes the big bucks while at the same time they exploit their help by working them long hours, giving them more than a one person workload and paying them barely enough to cover their basic living needs.*

Whether you are at the top or the bottom of the caste system makes little difference in the outcome because both are striving to make money and thus sacrificing their freedom in the process.

> *The American Dream was never about money but it has now evolved into that.*

The Solution

> *The solution on how to throw open the door that conceals possibilities is elementary and can be accomplished by anyone.*

The Eastern World has embraced the spiritual life but has denied the physical which is why they remain in poverty. Meanwhile the Western World has embraced the physical life and turned away from the spiritual aspect.

> *This is why the Western culture has problems with violence, drugs, stress and apathy toward their fellow man.*

The Eastern and Western cultures each have one side of the equation which if merged would create a very different world.

> *Picture a world that embraces each person's individuality with unconditional love and compassion, and without judgment: a world that treats everyone with kindness and fairness.*

It would mean that gangs, terrorists, wars, hate crimes

and the mental and emotional pain that many suffer from would be vanquished. I know your thinking, that this is a fairy tale place and it will never exist.

> *I say it can and will exist and I am personally doing everything that I can to ensure its creation.*

It begins and ends with you. You decide that you are going to develop yourself into the type of person that would live in that kind of world.

> *Simplify your life and switch your priorities from gathering everything outside you to nurturing the spiritual being within you.*

> *When we heal our bodies, minds, emotions and spirit we become whole and are able to achieve an internal peace.*

It is time for the average American to get in touch with their essences and to regain control of their lives from the government and the business world. We need to demand holistic care from our health care providers. Doctors and mental health workers only heal the manifested symptoms such as cancer and depression but they rarely seek to heal the individual as a whole.

Alternative therapies tend to heal with age old techniques such as acupuncture, energy work, massage therapy, etc., but renounce medical healing.

> *How much better would our health be if we combined mystical healing with scientific healing?*

An individual could go to one center and have everything they need in order to be fully healed. There are centers out there that do this but as of this writing insurance companies do not recognize the majority of alternative modalities, so only those who have money can afford to use the centers.

> *Until the culture changes it becomes the individual's responsibility to heal themselves holistically.*

This means that you must delve into self study on how to transform your entire life. Then your life becomes an example for others to follow.

> *The business community needs a wake-up call.*

They received one at the time unions were formed but then the unions themselves became exactly what they were fighting against. Where does this leave the average person? The focus of business has always been the bottom line but now they are starting to shift into quality and customer relations.

> *The core problem that remains is that employers treat their workers as a disposable resource, giving them little respect or compassion.*

The corporate world needs to quit playing the zero sum game of lose, lose and reconcile itself to the fact that employees are their most valuable resource.

> *This philosophy is on the cutting edge and it creates a win/win environment for everyone but it has to be a philosophy that is lived, not just a group of words written on paper to make the executives look good.*

We all need to think seriously about this next ideal.

> *There is more than enough of everything to go around.*

No person should ever be without a home, food or clothing. If we switch how we view prosperity we can improve the lifestyles of many and enhance the planet as well.

Individuals are destroying the rain forest so that they can feed their families. This affects the entire population on the planet, so why do we allow it to continue? Why don't we provide the individuals with food and housing and have them be the rain forest guardians?

> *Each country could supply the world with the service, product or resource that is within their realm to offer.*

No one country or person should be in control of the earth's basic natural resources such as fresh water, fertile soil or oxygen- producing forests because all life is dependent upon the use of those resources.

> *We must all unite together as one race and help one another to meet the basic needs of life.*

Again I am sure that you are thinking that this will never happen and what can one person do? Share your time, love and prosperity with those who are less fortunate than you. I am not speaking to the rich only here, everyone has something they can share even if it is only a smile or a nice word.

> *Opening yourself up to the possibilities that life has to offer is a giant step forward and is simple to do.*

Once you define in detail what you realistically need in your life to be content, fulfilled, and peaceful then you can put your energy into achieving your desires. The next step is to eliminate limitation and to develop your value system based on your beliefs.

> *When you understand why you believe what you do it becomes possible for you to live your beliefs, and thus you will begin to live your truth.*

Next you must identify what it is that you fear, then you need to heal your fears by confronting them and moving beyond them.

> *You must always look within for your balance, internal peace and joy because it all resides inside each and every individual who resides upon this planet.*

Finally as stated throughout this book, it all begins and ends with the individual.

> *One person can make a difference.*

When you choose to grow into a person who is loving, non-judgmental, compassionate and sharing you help to change the world around you and if everyone did this, think how it would alter the world. The possibilities are endless!

8

FINAL THOUGHTS

> *I am sure that you have found valuable information contained in this book and you might think incorporating it into your life could take the rest of your time here on Earth.*

It will take you as long as you choose for it to take. It could be a week, a year or even your entire lifetime.

You will have lessons as long as you live. I will use this chapter to touch on some topics that I feel are important and that might be of interest to you. They are diverse and are not mentioned in any particular order. Remember that there are as many paths as there are individuals.

> *Incorporate only the information that is aligned with your truth.*

Lessons

Okay, you now know that you cannot escape from lessons. You are going to find that your lessons are not always evident. You may be aware that you are in the middle of one, but unable to figure out what exactly it is about. Don't fret, there is nothing wrong with you.

> *It's much easier to see the lessons of others than to see your own.*

To continue your growth you must work with and embody every lesson.

> *When you are unable to figure your lesson out, become still and review the events occurring in your life.*

You should find something that appears out of alignment with you and that is what you need to focus on.

When you are experiencing a "bad" day figure out why you consider it "bad." Here is an example: If you are experiencing delays in aspects of your life, the lesson could be as simple as developing patience. It sounds easy, but I can assure you it's not.

Another thing you can do is find a teacher who has the ability to see clearly. He or she should be able to point you in the right direction, but he or she cannot do the work for you.

> *Lessons do not need to be hard and learned through strife.*

You can choose to have them presented with grace and ease, and in the energy of joy.

Also, as you progress your messages will come in a more subtle form. This is because you are more aware and no longer require the Universe to shout at you to get your attention.

> *Stay in the flow, relax and have patience, and you will move forward if it is your desire.*

Responsibility/Accountability

We need to discuss responsibility and accountability. This is where you practice harmlessness and love.

> *As your knowledge base increases you are held to a higher level of both responsibility and accountability.*

This only seems fair. If you disagree, think how we do this to our children the older they become.

> *If you choose to use your new found knowledge to manipulate another or to achieve an outcome out of selfishness, you will be called on it by the Universe.*

Each phase of your growth increases your personal power.

> *You will feel the strength that rises up from within you and with this power you are given greater responsibility and accountability.*

You are to live in harmlessness towards all, including yourself. Seek purity of your mind, body and spirit.

> *Every thought, word and deed must be in the energy of
> unselfish love.*

This is not to say that you will never have days where you think or say something negative, it just means that you must be alert.

> *If you happen to think a negative thought, cancel it,
> forgive yourself and release the moment.*

This is not as hard as it seems.

> *You have made the choice to grow, which means you have
> chosen to become a better person.*

You achieve this by being responsible for your life.

Intuition

Now let's look at intuition and psychic abilities.

> *How many of you wish to have psychic abilities, such as to
> see auras, predict the future, channel and the like?*

We are all capable of these feats but they are not as important as you would think. Many who have these abilities do not live in love and harmlessness. If you choose to develop any of the above abilities I suggest you find a book or a loving teacher on the particular subject you are interested in.

I caution you to not focus all of your energy on developing your psychic abilities but, we will discuss intuition. Everyone has intuition.

> *When you follow your intuition you are being psychic.*

To foster this all you need to do is go into your inner guidance and listen to what it is telling you.

> *I told you earlier that every answer to every question you have is contained within you.*

The easiest way to develop your intuition is to use it if the information is safe. You always have the ability to override your guidance. Ask yourself simple yes or no questions and follow the first answer you get. For example, ask "Should I go to the store now?" If you receive "yes" then go. If you received "no" then do not go.

> *As you make your questions tougher, really feel and listen for a response.*

Be of the mind set that you will receive a response. After a while you will be able to tap in to your intuition for all your answers.

> *If you have a "gut" feeling telling you to do something, follow it if it is safe and unselfish.*

Make sure you give gratitude after receiving your answers because intuition stops or fades without it.

> *Women tend to use their intuition more, because it comes from our feminine energy.*

When you use intuition your mind becomes upset because logic goes out the window. It's difficult to explain why you believe something when it is your intuition telling you, as others may not agree with your method, and you can't give a reasonable explanation.

> *My hunches, or intuitions, are seldom wrong— unexplainable, yes, but seldom wrong.*

Love

> *The most important thing I can impart to you is that love is the only thing that truly matters in this world and in the universe.*

You can aspire to be rich, famous, or even a good person, but unless love is embedded into your core being and shared with the world around you, nothing worthwhile has been achieved.

This is far from new information. Jesus and Buddha spoke of it, as have many others.

> *If every single individual on this planet practiced unconditional love we would be living in paradise.*

You do not wait for another to love you before you love them; this would not be unconditional. You do not need to like the person but you must always project unconditional love to them.

> *No matter what a person has done in his or her life, they still have a piece of God deep inside, and that is where you focus your love.*

The more love you give, the more you have to give.

> *You can never run out of love because it is limitless!*

Gratitude

Gratitude is also important.

> *When you rise in the morning be grateful for the new day and the new possibilities available to you.*

If you're in the middle of a crisis find something to be

grateful for. You may have to stretch yourself to find it, but there is always something good in your life no matter how small.

Many forget to be grateful when their life is going great. It's not that people are ungrateful for their good fortune, it's that they become caught up in everyday living and forget to say thank you. When things are not so swell in our life is when we think to talk to God.

> God would also like to hear from you when things are as you want them to be. Everyday say thanks!

Prayer and Meditation

Prayer is also used more often when we want something from God.

> I believe that it is okay to request things if that is your desire, but you will eventually find that everything you need is within you.

So why would you pray?

> You pray for guidance, awareness, to send love and healing to individuals and the world as a whole.

I pray that my will is aligned with God's will at all times. If you request something don't be so specific that you limit how it can be given to you.

> *Know that God knows your needs and desires and the best way to meet them.*

Prayer is simply talking to God and it can be done anywhere, any time.

> *It is good to develop a relationship with the Creator.*

> *Meditation is stilling your mind to listen for insight, inspiration, and guidance.*

When you first begin to meditate you will need to do it in a controlled environment. As you become better at it you will be able to do it anywhere and at anytime.

> *Eventually the goal is for your life to be a meditation. I think this means that you are able to hear your inner guidance at all times and that the needless mind chatter ceases to exist.*

Sharing

> *As you grow you are going to want all your friends and family to grow with you.*

You may be excited and decide to share your new found knowledge with everyone. It's fine to do but, be prepared for a less than enthusiastic response.

> *It is normal for you to want to share something that has created joy in you but, remember that we all grow at our own rate.*

Your friends and family may not be ready to hear your truths. Patience is important in this instance.

> *You never want to walk away from someone without giving them proper time to assimilate your new energy and decide if they want to grow with you.*

If you quietly wait, people you know and love will eventually recognize the changes in you and they will question you about it. This becomes your opening to share your truths with them.

Creating

> *You are the creator of your destiny and you can create a positive future or a negative one.*

Many individuals live their entire life in a state of panic and fear. Embracing fear can bring forth a negative future.

> Are you ready to step out of mass consciousness and seek your own truths?

Together we can create a world that is filled with peace and love!

> It is time for us all to decide that we will live in a world that honors all life forms.

It begins with you and me!

Paradox

Life is filled with paradoxes. I would like to share this one with you.

> To achieve total fulfillment and joy you must stand still in your essences and gather your nourishment from within.

You will discover a new appreciation for all the blessings given to you.

> When you search outside of yourself you gather things and people and quickly become complacent towards them because they cannot sustain you.

When you live the truth that everything you need is inside, there is no way you could ever take for granted the gifts of love and abundance given to you from the Universe.

This book has been a challenge for me and I hope a blessing for you.

> *The voyage into yourself will be one of your greatest accomplishments and the discoveries you will make are never ending.*

I am grateful for the opportunity to have shared what I believe to be truth with you. Good luck and good fortune on your journey!

APPENDIX

I have included a meditation for your Quiet Place. You can tape this meditation or memorize it. If you tape it be sure to leave space on the tape to allow you time to accomplish your task once you are in your Quiet Place.

> *You can go to your Quiet Place to find peace, to figure out a problem or to talk to a friend.*

Eventually you should be able to arrive at your Quiet Place without having to meditate deeply. It is a great place to go when you are in the throes of a stressful situation. You can go to your Quiet Place and regroup and re-energize yourself. You don't need to spend much time there—just long enough to relax.

Meditation: Creating Your Quiet Place

Begin by finding a comfortable position and closing your eyes. Next take 3 deep breaths. Breathe in deeply and slowly, then hold your breath to the count of 3, then slowly breathe out. Again breathe in, hold to 3 and breathe out. Last time—breathe in, hold...hold...hold, and breathe out.

Allow your body to begin to relax...Peace and love and safety are all around you...and you begin to relax. Feel the room filled with the White Light of protection and allow your body to soften and be quiet. Think peace and love...Peace and Love...Peace and Love...

I am going to count down now from 5 to 1 and when I reach the number 1 you will be deeply relaxed, feeling safe and loved and peaceful...5 You are becoming more relaxed, more and more relaxed...4 White Light fills the room and surrounds and permeates your body as you relax deeper and deeper...3 You feel your body becoming more deeply relaxed with each moment and when I reach the count of 1 you will feel deeply relaxed...2 You are almost there now, feeling relaxed and safe and loved, deeper and deeper, deeper and deeper...

And 1, Deeply relaxed now—feeling peaceful and protected and loved. Enjoy the feeling and allow your body to continue to relax and be peaceful.

You are very relaxed now and feeling wonderful. In your mind's eye begin to see that you are in a very beautiful place...your Quiet Place, at your favorite time of day. Begin to see it more and more clearly. Take time to enjoy it and notice details about it. Know that this is your Quiet Place—it is only for you and cannot be entered by anyone else unless they are specifically invited by you.

Walk around and see the beauty of your special place...notice the colors and the shapes and as you walk, smell the fragrances that are present—the flowers of the garden, the spring grass, the salt breezes from the ocean or the energized air of the mountains.

Feel the ground at your feet, the petals of the flowers, the clean, wetness of the water—whether it be pond, lake or ocean —and the comfortable warmth of the sun upon your skin.

Next reach down and pick some new spring grass and taste it or cup some water in your hand and taste that—so clear and clean.

And while you are doing these things listen and hear the songs of the birds, the waves breaking on the beach, the soft wind caressing you on your mountain top. What else can you hear?

Walk around your Quiet Place and as you do, continue to build it, to invent it. Make it more and more beautiful all the time. Know that every time you return here in meditation it will grow and change...it evolves in beauty as you do.

Somewhere in your Quiet Place, place a chair for your comfort. Let it be very soft and cozy...made of beautifully colored materials. Now see yourself surrounded by the white light of protection. Visualize your physical body sitting in the chair. Accept and unconditionally love your physical body as it is. You should have already decided what trait you have chosen to release. See the trait, give it form, color and texture. Now embrace the trait; hug it to you, thank it for doing the job it was created to do. In your mind or out loud tell the trait that it no longer serves you to keep it. Surround the trait with love, encase it in white light, then throw it up to the Universe. Watch it leave you and dissolve into space...Now visualize the void that has been created and fill it with a positive trait you wish to embody...(If you cannot think of a positive trait use Unconditional Love). Give it form, color and substance. Now visualize the new positive energy entering into you and filling the void. Feel the new energy and welcome it, embrace it to you. Relax and enjoy the peace that surrounds you.

Now prepare to finish. Take one last look around your Quiet Place. Memorize its beauty even though you know it may change. The memory will sustain you.

In a moment I will count from 1 to 3. When I reach the number 3—and not before—you will open your eyes, feeling refreshed, happy and relaxed. You will also remember everything that happened during your meditation. On the count of 3...
1... 2... 3!

(Please note: If you tape this meditation for use at bed time, replace the prompt that wakes you up with: "You are now done with your meditation. Enjoy your Quiet Place as you drift into a deep, restful, happy sleep. You will awaken in the morning feeling refreshed and rested and relaxed. Now sleep...")

*Repeat the above meditation replacing your physical body with your mental, emotional and then spiritual body.

Soul Talking

This technique is fabulous for releasing bottled up feelings. I learned it from Daniele DeVoe who channeled it during one of her meditation sessions.

> *When you need to talk to someone, but you know that they will not listen, or you are sure that it will turn into a shouting match, try Soul Talking.*

To do this all you need are two chairs and a place where you cannot be overheard. You sit in one of the chairs then call the other person's soul in and invite them to sit in the opposite chair. This may seem "out there," but I assure you that it works. Imagine that the individual is right in front of you and begin talking. Tell them everything that is on your mind, everything.

> *Talk until you can't think of one more word to say, then you need to take a deep breath and tell them you forgive them and love them and thank them for listening.*

Tell them good bye, just as if their physical presence was in your home.

> *There is only one rule and that is you must end Soul Talking in the energy of unconditional love and harmlessness.*

When you have finished you should feel that you have released your emotions that required releasing and you should feel a sense of peace and calm. If you don't then you probably did not verbalize everything that you needed to say and you should try it again. Do Soul Talking the next time you need to communicate with someone unreachable and you will be amazed at the results!

God bless!

ABOUT THE AUTHOR

Heartbroken, empty, no meaningful direction in her life, and months of "bad hair days," Kathryn turned within and uncovered her Soul's desire. Her journey of self-discovery led to a personal relationship with God and nature. She learned to move forward by embracing her lessons and seeing the humor of it all.

As a nurse executive, she was afforded the opportunity to interact with individuals who required not just physical healing, but emotional, mental, and spiritual healing as well. To accomplish her work of healing the whole person, she was compelled to break free from conventional constraints placed upon her by corporate America.

Embracing her truth, she left her secular job, became an ordained minister and created a business called "Living Balance" which provides the medium for her to aid others through her workshops, ministry, spiritual counseling and writing.

Living one's own truth is not always easy. Kathryn proves that it can be done by anyone who has the ambition and dedication to try. This book is refreshing, honest, user-friendly and written with conviction, insight and sincerity.